Rele

Christmas 2000

Dave

Released from the Snare

by
John Glass

Foreword by
Dr R.T. Kendall

alpha

Copyright © 2000 John Glass

First published in 2000 by Alpha

06 05 04 03 02 01 00   7 6 5 4 3 2 1

Alpha is an imprint of Paternoster Publishing,
PO Box 300, Carlisle, Cumbria, CA3 0QS, UK
and Paternoster Publishing USA
PO Box 1047, Waynesboro, GA 30830-2047
www.paternoster-publishing.com

British Library Cataloguing in Publication Data

A catalogue record for this book is available from the
British Library

ISBN 1-89893-884-9

Cover design by Campsie, Glasgow
Typeset by WestKey Ltd, Falmouth, Cornwall
Printed in Great Britain by Cox & Wyman Ltd,
Cardiff Road, Reading, Berkshire, RG1 8EX

Dedication

This book is dedicated to those I am privileged to work alongside in Elim at home and overseas: the national leadership team, ministers, missionaries and lay leaders alike. God is calling you to your destiny: 'free to fly'.

Contents

Foreword by Dr R.T. Kendall

Not long ago my friend Lyndon Bowring stood next to John Glass at the latter's former church in Scotland. Lyndon was there as a guest preacher. During the service there was a distraction, a child running down the aisle towards the platform. The child's mother went forward to bring the child back into the congregation. But this happened several times. John then whispered to Lyndon, 'I will have to take care of this'. He then went to the mother and said something to her which resulted in the child not going back up the aisle to the platform again.

But moments later John whispered to Lyndon, 'I did the wrong thing. The Spirit lifted off me after I spoke to the mother. I must go back to her and apologise.'

When Lyndon told me this, I immediately said that I would love to read the manuscript of John's book Lyndon had just told me about. For I had just completed a book on the subject of the sensitivity of the Spirit, and I only wish that I had had the above account to tell in my own book. But when I learned this about John Glass, it in a sense told me more about him than anything I could possibly want to know!

John Glass is the new General Superintendent of the Elim Pentecostal Church. He follows a line of succession of outstanding men of this century, two of whom I happen to know intimately. The first is Eldin Corsie, who became General Superintendent after being the Pastor of Kensington Temple in London. Elim would invite me to speak at their annual Bible Week and this gave me my first introduction to the people of the Elim Church. I don't know when I felt so at home in all my life. Eldin was succeeded by Wynne Lewis, who had previously succeeded Eldin at London's Kensington Temple. Wynne and I became close friends over the years. He too invited me to preach for the Elim Church. As a result of my friendship with Wynne I met Paul Cain. As a result of my friendship with the present pastor of Kensington Temple, Colin Dye, I met Rodney Howard-Browne. These men have all had a powerful influence on me, so I count it an honour to have a part in the ministry that will continue at this level, namely that of John Glass.

When you read this book you will see that the new leadership of the Elim Church is in good hands. It is one of the most refreshing and challenging books I have read in a long time. It even deals with the practical implications of leadership, the nitty-gritty of life not often talked about in a book. It could serve as a handbook for Christian leaders, but also an introduction to leadership that many laymen would do well to read - if only to get an insight into what a leader has to live with!

This book deserves wider circulation than that merely within the constituency of Elim. Pentecostal and non-pentecostal alike, charismatic and non-charismatic alike, Church of England and non-conformist alike – all will profit from reading this unusual book.

What a leader is as a person is more important than what he says and does. This is why I mention the account above which shows how sensitive the author of this book is to the Holy Spirit – and to the 'lifting of the Spirit', as he puts it. It is important to recognise the presence of God, equally important to recognise his absence. This is just a hint of the kind of man who has written this book and why I am delighted to recommend it.

R.T. Kendall

Introduction

Having crossed the threshold into a new millennium, the Church has to evaluate what it has done with the past two thousand years. Whilst it is certain that multiplied millions have come to faith in Christ during this time, and there are certainly current flash-points of revival across the globe, for the most part the Church in the western hemisphere has little to congratulate itself about.

Christians hungry for revival have prayed fervently, church-growth specialists have analysed cities demographically, new initiatives have been planned and launched, but the harvest has been sparse.

This book contends that, while the Church grapples with God, imploring him to 'do something new', the reality is that many Christians have become ensnared, rendering themselves immobile. Sometimes it is not God that needs to move but us.

Imagine for a moment a fox whose object it is to run across an open field to the cover of woods where its vixen and cubs are waiting. To the animal the field is incidental – little more than a route to be traversed.

The fox races towards its destination oblivious to the fact that the field conceals a trap. As the snare snaps shut, all vision vanishes and the focus shifts to present pain.

Those who have found that their once-held dream has died and their goals have gone will find, in the pages that follow, the way out of their snare. Destiny and dream are about to come alive again.

Others, especially those who have recently come to faith, can use this book as a bomb disposal expert might examine a field that had previously been sown with mines but which now has been clearly plotted and charted. Why worry about being extricated from a trap that you are able to avoid?

The Bible assumes that the believer is someone who should be continually making progress. Before people were ever known as Christians, they were designated as the community of 'The Way' whose walk was by faith and not by sight. They did not stumble on their path by chance but rather had made a choice to be there. The route was as clear as their trust in the Master who would lead them. Their destination was assured. If the enemy of their souls could not deter them from making a decision to travel, he would be sure to do all in his power to prevent them making progress.

The popular British television programme, *The Cook Report*, dedicated to exposing fraud and deception at home and abroad, on one occasion did an exposure on the import of exotic birds. The opening shots portrayed these beautiful creatures in their natural habitat. The cameras traced them soaring over golden beaches and darting across azure sea and sky into tropical forests which were as close to paradise as the human mind could conceive. They were the very icons of freedom.

Concealed lenses then disclosed to the viewers the method that modern poachers use to ensnare their unsuspecting prey. Little had changed from the methods employed three thousand years ago by biblical fowlers. Savage nets, hung high between the branches, trapped the beautiful birds and brought them hurtling to the ground.

Animal lovers watched aghast as they saw the crude methods used to clip the wings of the fallen bird. Once caught, they would never be allowed to soar again in the habitat for which they had been created.

Imagine, if you will, two birds on adjacent perches, one with wings that have been clipped and the other with pinions intact. A first glance would make it almost impossible to know one from another. They may look identical and make the same noises and calls. Both may be able to flutter their wings to a degree. The truth will only emerge at the moment they attempt to fly.

Now picture two Christians sitting side by side in a pew. Outwardly they are indistinguishable. Both have been saved for the same length of time. Each of them is faithful in attendance and tithing and has similar gifts. When it comes to worship both can assume similar postures in praise. The only way we will know which one has been caught in a fowler's snare is at the point that they endeavour to 'fly' – to experience the destiny that they have been created for.

If you are reading this and feel that you have been spiritually grounded – hope is not lost. You can soar again. Your wings can be healed. You will fly!

Surely he will save you from the fowler's snare and from the deadly pestilence. He will cover you with his feathers, and under his wings you will find refuge; his faithfulness will be your shield and rampart (Ps. 91:3,4).

1

The Fear of Man

Fear of man will prove to be a snare, but whoever trusts in the LORD is kept safe (Prov. 29:25).

Fear to change

Searching a Christian bookstore for a title on the subject of fear will reveal a multitude of choices. Many of these books will be worthy and helpful and all of them written from a premise that fear is bad for you and must be eradicated at all cost. This is not entirely true, for fear is an emotion created by God. In its best sense it acts as a warning system. How safe would a child be who has no fear of fire or of traffic?

Spiritually, all the best blessings that some would long for, stem from a healthy 'fear of God'. So much so that the Scripture says, 'The fear of the Lord is the beginning of wisdom'.[1] Longevity, material prosperity, honour, even church growth and the ability to overcome evil stem from this disposition.[2]

Whilst the fear of God is a positive attribute, few spiritual states are as immobilising as the fear of man.

Why is it that a person is reluctant to pray publicly for the first time? It is not because of a fear of God, but rather the anxiety that their prayer might not compare favourably with the articulate offering of another church member. Why are we reticent to witness? A fear of God has nothing to do with it but rather the unwillingness to be perceived as a crank or religious eccentric. Extend the example to cover the use of spiritual gifts, exterior modes of worship and volunteering for service and we quickly realize that these are not petty distractions of the Enemy. They are a major weapon in his armoury against the child of God.

We will look at two case histories where the names are changed but the accounts are taken from real life.

Fiona's story

Fiona is approaching middle-age and has been in the church several years. Each Sunday night after the evening service she joins her circle of friends for supper. In the past, the form of service in her church has been as comfortable as it has been predictable. Over the past few months however things have begun to change – most noticeably in the style of worship.

This gives Fiona's small circle something to get their teeth into. The lack of predictability has bred a sense of insecurity. 'If we can't explain it then we must blame it'; 'If this is right then why is it not happening to us? We're every bit as good as they are'; 'vollies from the valley syndrome'[3] is beginning to emerge and Fiona finds herself as 'caught up' in it as everyone else. She has however become oblivious to the fact that her fellowship circle is quickly becoming a clique and in danger of the incestuous bonding that inevitably unites around a negative.[4]

The problem is that Fiona is acutely aware that her life is spiritually empty. There are times when she would long with all her heart to be in the middle of all that God is doing in the lives of others. Time after time she craves to make her way to the front, but the thought of the taunt of friends, and breaking ranks with her circle, has delineated her personal snare. Only after a mammoth and painful struggle is she able to extricate herself.[5] Emancipation was only attainable at the point that her fear of offending God overtook her fear of offending her friends.

In some situations a 'fear of man' not only has the potential to rob us of spiritual fruitfulness but can also be capable of affecting a person's eternal destiny. Our next account reveals how fear and love can coexist as parallel jaws of this deadly trap.

The fiancée

My maternal grandfather, John Woodhead, was one of the earliest pentecostal evangelists in the days when George and Stephen Jefferies were establishing the modern Pentecostal Movement. He pioneered over twenty churches and, towards the end of his ministry, was to become the President of the Elim churches. In the 40s and 50s it would be usual for him to conduct tent campaigns in large marquees – it was in such a venue that I came to faith in Christ as a boy.

It was on one such occasion that an engaged couple attended the meetings. When the gospel appeal was made for those who wished to surrender their lives to Christ, the young lady turned to her fiancé and whispered to him, as she edged out of her seat, that she felt that she must go forward. His response was immediate. Only barely sustaining a whisper, he announced in no uncertain terms that if she were to make her way to the front she would, by that act, end the relationship. The wedding would be off. The snare had been set and the young woman regained her seat.

On the closing night of the crusade, having attended several times, a similar scenario was acted out. On this occasion however the work of the Holy Spirit on her life prevailed over every other coercion. She made her way forward to the front with the words, 'I love you and don't want to lose you, but if you won't come to heaven with me, then I'm not going to go to hell with you.'

This account gives us a first insight into escaping spiritual snares. One hand on the teeth of the trap has to be ours. There must be a firm act of our will. We must want to be free. The grip on the other jaw has to be God's. As the psalmist said,

'My eyes are ever on the Lord, for only he will release my feet from the snare.'[6]

I now want to say a word to leaders; though other readers should not skip this section. Firstly, I am not assuming a leader only to be someone in what is sometimes referred to as 'full-time service'. If you are an elder, youth worker, cell-group leader or parent, many of the principles will be applicable to you. Secondly, this section may encourage you to pray more earnestly for those to whom you look for spiritual covering in your local fellowship.

When a Christian becomes caught in a snare the results, though devastating, may affect only the individual concerned. When a leader grinds to a halt there is a very real danger that many of those who are following him or her are similarly immobilised. When the leader is motionless he ceases to be a guide and has become merely a signpost. No one ever followed a parked car.

When I was a young man in my final year at theological college a senior minister, aware that I was shortly to be appointed to a pastorate, indicated that God had given him a word for me. I was excited and, in the split second between this revelation and the one that was to come, I wondered what could possibly be the content of this anointed disclosure. Would it give some prophetic insight into my long-term future? Would it portend some gifting of which I was currently unaware? This was his word: 'John, the Lord would say to you – Jeremiah 1:7–9' and with that he went away.

I must confess to gross disappointment. Before I even consulted the text, I was immediately apprehensive of anything that was going to emanate out of the book of Jeremiah – perhaps only Lamentations could have been worse.

I read the text in my room and, though more than thirty years of pastoral ministry have passed, I still have reason to remember and be grateful for them. They were given to me in the Authorised Version so it is that from which I quote:

> The Lord said unto me, Say not, I am a child: for thou shalt go to all that I shall send thee, and whatsoever I command thee thou shalt speak. Be not afraid of their faces: for I am with thee to deliver thee, saith the Lord (Jer. 1:7–9).

'Be not afraid of their faces'. It was not what I had expected, but this experienced warrior knew that a young man would one day need to be able to overcome the fear of man and deal with one of the deadliest weapons in the Enemy's armoury – intimidation.

Many years later, as a Regional Superintendent within the denomination to which I belong, I became concerned about a small church that was not only static numerically, but experiencing an inordinate turnover of pastors. Young men would come, become discouraged, and then seek a new appointment.

I discovered that within the small fellowship there was a man who was exercising an undue and intimidating influence over the church. It further transpired that he was one of the main contributors to the church finances. It seemed that when any pastor was inclined to make a change to something in the life of the fellowship that did not synchronise precisely with his narrow prejudices, he would threaten to withdraw his financial support. When, some time later, a minister was inducted who was not dependent on the church for his income, the power base of this controlling spirit was undermined and he left the fellowship in search of easier prey.

This eventuality solved the problem for the church but not for the leaders who had previously left. You cannot escape a snare by moving yourself geographically, even though, like the psalmist, you are tempted to say, 'Oh, that I had the wings of a dove! I would fly away and be at rest.'

Like balls and chains on prisoners of an earlier era, snares are painfully portable. They reside in the spirit, not in the circumstance. There are snares that hold you fast and snares, like these, that slow you down. To be free in your leadership you must overcome the intimidating fear of man.

Fear to discipline

During my time in Scotland I had the privilege of pioneering a number of congregations. Starting with a small group of between six and twelve people, we would begin a home cell and later book a school or hotel in which to hold the services.

On one such occasion, when meeting in a hotel, I noticed a young couple who had not attended before. Speaking to them afterwards I enquired as to whether they lived in the city or were in the area on holiday. They explained that they lived in the locality and then proceeded to enthuse about the service. They came quickly to the conclusion that this was just the place that they had been looking for, and the church that they wanted to make their spiritual home. Feeling that they were coming to this conclusion too quickly, I dug a little deeper and in doing so unearthed the following story.

It transpired that they belonged to another church in the area and had had a disagreement with the leadership of the fellowship. They went on to relate that they were planning to marry and had made a decision to sell one of their flats and move in with each other. They had come to this conclusion, they assured me, purely on economic grounds and, though living in the same accommodation, would not be living together as man and wife. The elders of their church had suggested that, even if they kept to this agreement, it was a bad testimony both for them and the church.

I was then regaled with a lengthy list of their gifts and graces for which they assumed our embryonic congregation should be grateful and was asked, though only rhetorically, whether I didn't think their former church narrow-minded and untrusting? I responded to the effect that, while not questioning their many talents, I had to agree entirely with their current leaders. I was of the opinion that they should return and submit to the covering of a group of leaders for which they should be eternally grateful. I never saw them again.

Neither their church nor mine was willing to lower its standards for fear of losing people – however gifted they may have been. As I have mentioned in a previous book, to build any church on a basis that

lacks integrity is to build termites into the foundation.
Such a group may not collapse in the short term but its
demise is guaranteed. This is one of the reasons why
many churches stay the same size for generations.
They were not birthed properly.

Leaders with an inordinate desire to please people
will find themselves in a snare from which only courage and a sound self-image will extricate them. In my
study at home hangs a print that shows the hands of
an orchestral conductor holding a baton. The caption
reads, 'To lead a symphony you may occasionally
have to turn your back on the crowd.'

The story is told of an old man who was travelling
with a child and a donkey. Passing the first village the
man led the donkey while the child walked. The inhabitants suggested that he was stupid for not riding
the sturdy beast. So, in order to please the crowd he
climbed on. Entering the next town the people said he
was quite obviously a selfish person – riding while the
child was forced to walk. To resolve the matter on the
next stage of his journey he put the boy on the donkey.
Now he was criticized for encouraging laziness in the
child. In desperation they both mounted the beast
only to be castigated for cruelly subjecting the animal
to intolerable stress. The man and the child were last
seen carrying the donkey between them.

Fear of reality

In the seven years prior to my call to serve the Elim
churches as General Superintendent, my ministry
was based at the Church of God in Kilsyth. An

incident that occurred prior to my assuming the pastorate highlights what happens when individuals choose to resist the snare of the fear of man.

Kilsyth Church of God is the longest established Pentecostal congregation in Scotland. It has a remarkable history as does the town itself which, although less than ten thousand in population has witnessed three major revivals in the past two hundred and fifty years.[8] Apart from being situated on one of the most revival-soaked portions of the planet, there were two other things that set the church apart from a normal Pentecostal congregation. One was that the church had been independent and, as far as some were concerned, fiercely so. The other was that in its long history it had never had a salaried minister. It operated on Brethren lines with a group of elders: one of which was designated a presiding elder or president. For much of its history this had worked well: especially under the fine spiritual leadership of men such as Harry Tee[9] and James Gibson. The church however had now reached a point when it was experiencing a period of decline both spiritually and numerically.

It was into this context that the current president John Stark, a godly man of high integrity, invited two people to preach at the annual convention. They were Warwick Shenton and Paul Weaver, both of whom would later hold office as General Superintendent within the Assemblies of God UK.

It was Warwick, before he died, who related to me the dilemma which faced them. Should they preach good convention sermons, or should they confront the church with the truth of their situation? The latter choice carried the possibility of forever alienating them from the people and even carried a chance of causing fundamental dissension within the church. Those who know these men, whom I number among my closest friends, will have no doubt about the decision that they made. What eventually took place shows what can happen when leaders fear displeasing God more than they fear offending people.

The result was that, as soon as the convention concluded, the leaders called a church business meeting. The agenda did not call for censure but rather posed a single question: 'How do we put into practice, as the people of God, those things that have been spoken into our lives in recent ministry?' Oh that all preaching carried with it such an anointed aftermath.

The church had come to the conclusion that, through its isolation, it had become detached from the way the Spirit of God was moving in the nation. It resolved to come under the authority of a body of people who would give them spiritual covering.[10] They also had the humility to acknowledge that, at the retiring of their current president, there was no one present with the gifting to guide them to their destiny as a cutting-edge spirit-filled church.

Because two men refused to 'play to the gallery', or massage their own egos, a good church was set on course to a new future.

A good self-image

Some evangelicals are quick to recoil from the mention of 'image' in any form. To them it smacks of a self-assurance that borders on pride or arrogance. While agreeing that these traits should never be part of a Christian's profile, the fact remains that a damaged self-image is one of the most tempting baits that lure the victim into the snare that the Bible calls 'the fear of man'.

Earlier in the chapter I mentioned my grandfather who was a well-known minister within our denomination. The downside to this, as far as I was concerned, was that as a teenager I was very often introduced to people not by my own name but as 'the grandson of John Woodhead'. I never saw this as a particular problem at the time but later, when entering the ministry, I was continually conscious of a name that I concluded I had to live up to. I often felt, possibly wrongly, that comparisons were being made. I only fully realized how pronounced this complex had become when, as a young minister, I attended a large convention.

I set out to walk from the rear of the crowded hall towards an area located at the front of the auditorium. As I made my way down the aisle I noticed an internationally-known speaker heading in my direction and who, as it happened, was a close friend of my grandfather. What if he greeted me and I made some banal reply? Assuming that he had not caught sight of me I retraced my steps, left the building and, despite torrential rain lashing the streets, walked around the outside of the building and re-entered at a door to the rear. As I stood soaking, both rain and truth began slowly to seep in. I made a decision that day, for better or worse, that it was time to be myself.

This account will possibly appear ridiculous to everyone except those who have known the challenge of a poor self-image.

It was Rabbi Zusya who said, 'When I stand before God I will not be asked, "Why were you not Moses" but, "Why were you not Zusya?" '

It would be wrong to assume that only the young and inexperienced seek to mask an undeveloped or damaged self-awareness. It is said that American President Abraham Lincoln grew the beard by which he was so instantly recognized, because a little girl had written to him to say that it was a pity that her leader was not a handsome man.

It is certainly right that we should 'not think of ourselves more highly than we ought' but how highly ought we to think? While pride exalts a person beyond reality, false humility can debase another beyond usefulness. When James exhorts us to love our neighbour as ourselves, he starts with the assumption that we are comfortable with who God has already made us. It is out of that bedrock of wholeness that we are able to speak securely into the lives of others. Hurt people hurt people – whole people heal people.

2

Wrong Priorities

They mingled with the nations and adopted their
customs. They worshipped their idols which became a
snare to them (Ps. 106:35–36).

Spiritual pollution

It had been a hectic month and I was wondering, as
my plane approached San Francisco airport, why I
had accepted this particular ministry invitation. I
had never met the minister nor did I know anything
about the church that I was about to visit. I had been
booked in for a week's meetings on the recommen-
dation of a close friend of mine. There was one other
thing I did not know about this trip – something was
about to happen that would change the direction of
my life and ministry for ever.

It took another plane trip out of San Francisco to
Monterey and then a journey by road before I eventually came to my destination, Salinas, California.
Arriving at the church I was met by the pastors. They
were a husband and wife team in their seventies.

During the opening service a number of things immediately struck me as strange. The first was that, despite the age of the leaders, the church was packed to the doors with young couples and their children. Next I noticed that, as far as the service was concerned, they were doing everything wrong: the music was dated and the whole ethos of the church appeared to be light years away from being anything approaching 'cutting edge'. My other observation was that the church was in a revival that I was later to find out had been going on for four years. The meetings were packed every night of the week and I longed to discover the key. The presence of God in the place was awesome and everyone, including the children, was worshipping, interceding and often weeping before the Lord.

The following day I was asked to speak at the open assembly of their church school. I had two questions: how long did they want me to speak, and what was the age group that I would be addressing? I was staggered to learn that they wanted me to speak for at least an hour to an age range of from seven to seventeen. I suggested, as politely as I could, that it was not possible to cater for such a wide spectrum in one session. My protestations fell on deaf ears and I was shortly to find out why.

The pupils filed into the hall, youngest first, until all the older students had found their place and everyone was assembled. Then the headmaster, with a single clap of his hands, announced, 'Let's worship'. I must confess that my expectation was that a piano would strike up some predictable children's hymn. Instead the whole place began shouting praise in English and in tongues. Not one of the students appeared to be uninvolved and, for what seemed to be an eternity, I watched in awe as even the youngest raised their hands and called upon the Lord. I had witnessed some scenes like this in Africa but never in cynical and 'cool' California.

I was impatient to elicit from the pastor the reason for this remarkable manifestation of grace upon the church so, during the worship time in the evening service, I sought out his secret. I half anticipated that it would include a period of prolonged prayer and fasting or visiting ministry that had acted as a charismatic catalyst to bring about such remarkable change.

He waved his arm across his congregation of young families and to my surprise simply said, 'Not one of these people has a television in their home.' I waited for something more, but nothing more was offered.

It was then that my mind went back to the week prior to my trip. My wife Marilyn and I had been sitting watching the least innocuous of the 'soaps' when I had made the comment, 'You know, half of this programme is set in a pub and the other half in a betting shop; most of the couples are living together outside of marriage, and on Sunday I will probably be speaking against most of the values that are represented here – yet this is how we are using our precious recreational time.'

On the plane back to the UK I took out a secular book that had been given to me by a member of the church. A few minutes into the flight the young man in the adjacent seat inquired as to what I was reading.

I felt almost embarrassed to admit, at the dawn of the twenty-first century, that its title was, *Four Arguments against Television*. 'The reason I asked', he said, 'was because your reading matter is not greatly dissimilar from mine' and, tilting the spine of his paperback he revealed that he was reading a book on the same subject.

It turned out that he was a newly qualified doctor of medicine who was soon to be married, and went on to relate that he and his fiancée had resolved not to bring a television into their home for at least the first year of their new relationship. I came instantly to the conclusion that God may be trying to tell me something.

When I returned to my church I recounted my experiences and announced that I was about to embark on a three-month television fast that would even include the watching of the news. I invited any-one who wished to join me, for all or part of this time, to do so. I did not ask our people to 'sign up' for this venture as, in my experience, it is all too easy for things of this nature to degenerate into religious acts and cold duty.

The results in my personal life were dramatic: an increased sense of intimacy with God, the ability to hear God's voice more acutely in both purpose and direction, a deeper exercise of spiritual gifts – especially those of revelation.

There is little wonder that those who have been watching a film or video until late on Saturday night, whose plot may be murder or adultery, have some struggle getting into an attitude of worship in church on a Sunday morning. We should not be surprised that our teenagers are accepting sex outside of marriage as the norm when, in a soap, film or drama the words, 'Let's go to bed' are hardly ever uttered in the context of a relationship between husband and wife.

We are rightly conscious of what we eat knowing that our diet is inseparably linked to our health. The current debate about genetically modified food flags up the possibility that what we take into the food chain today could have calamitous consequences both on individuals and society in the future.

Given this awareness in a biological context there is surely a need to heed the warning alarm that awakens us to a need for vigilance over our spiritual safety. One wonders at the wisdom of Christian parents who provide unsupervised TV sets in the bedrooms of even their smallest children. Does not the argument that 'Everyone does it these days' tune more into the 'fear of man' than any other siren sound?

It is the insidious subtlety of Satan's strategy that makes it so menacing. The *modus operandi* of 'the Prince of the power of the air' towards the individual has some parallel with those who are involved in extraterrestrial combat of a technological nature. It is easier to soft-kill a satellite by distorting and corrupting the information that it receives than it is physically to shoot it down.

Who can expect to be healthy who insists on drinking from a polluted stream? To use another analogy: our eyes have become used to the dark and our spirits have subsequently become desensitised to the vision of God.

From time to time I have shared the account of my trip to Salinas when I have spoken at leaders' meetings and seminars. On several occasions I have received letters from ministers who have related the powerful effect that has taken place in their lives when they committed to a fast of this nature.[1]

During a television and media fast we do not suggest that the time saved has to be used for increased prayer and Bible study. What is every bit as important is husbands and wives spending quality time with one another and their children. Those who engage in it find that the fast does not simply cut off the flow of pollution; it stimulates the health of those areas of family life that have previously experienced atrophy through lack of use.

The Apostle Paul understood the need for a clear and healthy mind when he wrote to the Church at Philippi:

> Brothers, whatever is true, whatever is noble, whatever is right, whatever is pure, whatever is lovely, whatever is admirable – if anything is excellent or praiseworthy – think about such things (Phil. 4:8).

There is always a fear in some that, if they take a position such as this over television, others may consider them to be taking a super-spiritual stance.

Apart from the danger that we have previously noted about the 'fear of man', the opposite is in fact the case. When I was in Florida Dr Michael Brown, who is part of the ministry team in the Assemblies of God Church in Pensacola, related that when he checks into a hotel he requests that they remove the television set from his room prior to arrival. If they refuse to do so he goes elsewhere. He added that he does this, not because he considers himself more sanctified than other people, but because he has a healthy awareness of his own humanity.

Possessions

In the same way that we did not remove television sets from our home, but chose to be more acutely committed to watching what we watch, in this section I am not advocating that we dispense with all but essential material goods in order to be emancipated from them. To be free, means to ensure that our lives are liberated from a bondage to conspicuous consumption. I am writing this book from our home situated overlooking one of the most beautiful parts of Britain and for which we are continually grateful to God. Possessions do not become wrong when we possess them. They become wrong when they possess us – but possess us they most certainly can.

Consumerism, like all addictions, is a spiritual problem. Few people in their rational moments really believe that owning more things creates a greater sense of security. All of us know that money is not a panacea for every ill. Two of the world's richest men emphasise the point all too poignantly.

Howard Hughes left a legacy of a billion pounds but spent the last ten years of his life as a recluse. John Paul Getty was married and divorced five times and his eldest son died an alcoholic.

We have to ask ourselves who is the richer: the man who is wealthy and craves more or the poorer man who is content with what he has?

We live in a culture that says that it is essential to look good, feel good and make good. It was Eve, the first consumer, who fell for the lie that God was holding back from her something that was essential for her satisfaction.

Rudyard Kipling when addressing a graduate medical class at McGill University said, 'You will go out from here and no doubt make a lot of money. One day you will meet someone for whom that means very little. Then you will realize how poor you really are.'

From another perspective, R.E. Byrd, compiling his log while alone for months in the Antarctic wrote, 'I am learning that a man can live profoundly without masses of things.'

Both of them understood that standard of living is not the same as quality of life. It was David Livingstone who said, 'I place no value on anything except in its relationship to the Kingdom of God'. He was echoing the sentiments of Augustine who declared, 'All plenty that is not God, is poverty to me.'

Perhaps what we call the 'high cost of living' should more accurately be termed, 'the cost of high living':

But godliness with contentment is great gain. For we brought nothing into the world, and we can take nothing out of it. But if we have food and clothing, we will be content with that. People who want to get rich fall into temptation and a trap and into many foolish and harmful desires that plunge men into ruin and destruction.[2]

If materialism were the Devil then advertising would be his prophet. It is advertising that markets merchandise, having first turned it into images and visions. Charles Revlon of Revlon says, 'In the laboratory I make cosmetics. In the store I sell dreams.'

The seduction of the designer label gives an illogical sense of value to the individual who contrives to convince us that by possessing the product, she has in some sense, 'arrived'. In 1992 Michael Jordan received \$20 million for promoting Nike trainers. That was more than the entire annual payroll of the Indonesian factory that made them.

Of the six billion people on our planet 3.6 billion have neither cash nor credit. Those of us that do would appear to be working harder and harder to obtain those things that we have come to believe give us 'added value'. More and more of us are working for our possessions rather than the other way around. It has been calculated that 25% of the teachings of Jesus are focussed on our attitudes to what we own.

Richard Foster in his classic *Celebration of Discipline* makes a list of those things that hone the teeth on this particular snare.[3] I have selected just seven:

• Stop trying to impress people with your clothes and impress them with your life

- Reject anything that is producing an addiction in you
- Develop a habit of giving things away
- Refuse to be propagandised by the custodians of modern gadgetry
- Learn to enjoy things without owning them
- Develop a deeper appreciation for creation
- Look with a healthy skepticism at offered credit

All this poses the question, 'If I extricate myself from this snare, what then am I free to do?' The obvious answer may be that we are released from the pressure to possess or the crippling controls of credit and interest rates.

At the beginning of this section I made a plea for balance. I would be the last to add fuel to any fire of condemnation felt by those who have been blessed with material abundance. The message is simply that there has to be some symmetry between prosperity on one hand and responsibility on the other. There are some that handle this fiscal equilibrium with consummate poise.

One such person is a friend of mine who would be considered, by any standards, to have achieved significant financial success. In the view of those who know him, this has been earned through prudent investment based in a business that exudes excellence, integrity and service. His raison d'être is to release resources into ministries that will advance the Kingdom of God.

Part of his wide portfolio of interests is the ownership of a number of franchises that market cars in the upper echelons of the motor industry. When the customer takes delivery of their vehicle they will find in the glove compartment, adjacent to the manufacturer's manuals, a beautifully produced booklet entitled, 'A Word to the Wise'. In its 87 pages it divides the book of Proverbs into sections that deal with day to day living and concludes with a section on the way of salvation. On the back cover they will find these words:

> There are many people today who spend a considerable amount of money and effort in the search for successful living. This booklet reveals God's way – key spiritual principles that build up from the inside, rather than those that simply create an illusion of apparent confidence. If appropriated and lived by, these principles will totally transform your life.

Position

The human race shares a number of traits with the animal kingdom. Some attributes are essential for the procreation and preservation of the species – sexuality and care for the young being obvious examples. Other propensities are unhelpful crossovers within God's creation and number amongst the worst manifestations of what the Scripture refers to as 'the flesh'. Territorialism is a case in point.

Our two Siamese cats exemplify what I mean. As soon as we moved to the house in which we currently live, the male cat was quick to work out his territory. The signals were transmitted chemically through scent, and enforced materially by his physical presence as he boldly patrolled the perimeters of his new domain. Woe betide any cat that wandered either purposefully or inadvertently into his self-designated kingdom.

In the first few weeks there were a few trials of strength when fur would fly. More often than not the locked gaze and guttural hiss made actual violence unnecessary and encroaching infidels were soon sent packing with lowered eyes, and tails between their legs. Boundaries had been established. The new incumbent was secure. The rest of the local feline community too knew where they stood, as presumably they too had demarcations of their own that they considered similarly sacrosanct.

Humans are little different from animals in regards to territoriality. My encounter with a furious woman on a Welsh doorstep is a case in point. It occurred over twenty-five years ago but it is as fresh in my mind as if it were yesterday. I was a young pastor who had set about to do some house-to-house visitation. It became apparent that the explosion of the woman's anger had been detonated by my innocent use of the word 'church'. This was an organization, she informed me, that had inflicted upon her untold suffering and, though years had now passed, she was still reeling from the cruel blows that had rained down upon her during this traumatic episode of her life. The Spielberg-like build up to this epic was so intense I was fervently praying that I might be spared the horrific details. My prayers were to go unanswered.

It took only a few minutes for the full facts to be disgorged. When eventually the storm had blown

itself out I stood on the step speechless. It transpired
that this woman's responsibility had been to arrange
flowers on the church altar – a function she had
fulfilled for many years. One Sunday morning, her
duties completed, the vicar's wife entered the church
and, as she passed the floral display, had the
temerity to pause and adjust the ferns. This flagrant
incursion into the domain of the flower-arranger
was clearly only on a par with Hitler's invasion of
Poland and, in consequence, I was left with the
dramatic declaration, '. . . So I said to myself, well if
that's Christianity I will never darken the door of a
church again.' A territory had been transgressed.

A friend related to me the account of his visit to a
church while on holiday. The building, he informed
me, seated over six hundred, though that morning
there were only around fifty people present.

Just as the service was about to commence he was
aware of being prodded on the shoulder by two
irritated latecomers who, though there were
hundreds of chairs to choose from, made it clear that
my friends were sitting in their seats and, 'Would
they kindly move?'. No thought was given to the
visitors nor did it ever occur to them that these
people, instead of being the mature believers that
they were, might be non-Christians on their first visit
to a church service.

That such examples are mercifully rare should not
dull our senses to the insidious presence of the
neurotically guarded territory.

Territorialism can be found in the person who
looks with suspicion upon any semblance of
emerging talent in the church lest it should over-

shadow them or their 'gift'. It is present when musicians jealously guard their 'ministry' and are threatened when younger or more gifted people rise from within the church.

Most wars, industrial or national, are fought over territorial issues. Most church conflicts are skirmishes about power and control. Ask a machete-wielding soldier in Rwanda, a sniper in Bosnia or a suicide bomber in the Golan Heights what they are fighting over and, though their culture and colour may be different, the common denominator is most likely to be territory.

Probably the worst leader in the early church was Diotrephes. The story is presented to us in the Third Epistle of John. The Apostle wrote to him to say that he felt it right to minister at his fellowship. God had given him a word for the group.

Diotrephes would have none of it and told him in no uncertain terms to keep off his patch. Eventually people in the church heard about the rebuff and questioned their pastor about it. Diotrephes' retort was double-barrelled. The first salvo was one of vicious invective against the ministry and morals of John. The second came in the form of a threat to excommunicate anyone who raised the subject again. The literal translation of the name Diotrephes means 'nourished by Jove' (the Greek god Zeus or the Roman god Jupiter). Zeus was called 'guardian of law, defender of truth', the epitome of the religious spirit. In verse 11 of his third epistle, John designates Diotrephes a man inspired by evil.

If conflict were the only cause of territorialism that would be bad enough. The tragedy is that, in this case, the whole fellowship was affected and stunted by the action of one of its leaders. There can be no successful advancement into the Devil's territory (the only conflict the Church has been commissioned to conduct) if there are battles over borders between believers.

One of the primary blessings that hallmark the current move of the Holy Spirit is the dismantling of walls of exclusion between churches and denominations. The coming together of congregations in towns and cities for concerted prayer is one evidence of this barrier-breaking development. It is also evidenced in the willingness of denominational leaders to co-operate with one another, not out of coercion or duty, but out of a desire for genuine relationship. Today there is a new desire for unity, and it is awakened by the Spirit of God.

When the tribes were allocated their inheritance in the Promised Land it was God, not their colonial ego, that apportioned to them what was allotted. When they had previously camped in the wilderness there were few disputes between them because the tabernacle, and not their personal agendas, was their focal point. God ordained that the tabernacle, the symbol of his special presence, should always be in the centre of the camp.

Though our denominational tribes may remain distinct, and we retain our individual emphasis and identity, spiritual union is still secured wherever God's Kingdom is the primary focus. Dan does need to merge with Asher, or Gad with Naphtali, for this to be accomplished.

When territorial boundaries are dismantled or shared, something happens in the realm of the Spirit. This is true whether the focus is local or national, personal or denominational. It is the precursor of blessing.

How good and pleasant it is when brothers live together in unity! It is like precious oil poured on the head, running down on the beard, running down on Aaron's beard, down upon the collar of his robes. It is as if the dew of Hermon were falling on Mount Zion. For there the LORD bestows his blessing, even life for evermore (Ps. 133).

Inappropriate Relationships

The seventh sin God hates

I was in the middle of a preaching itinerary and the person driving me to the Sunday morning venue had lost his way. In consequence I arrived at the church just as the meeting was commencing. I had never visited this fellowship before nor had I met the pastor previously.

Well into my message I felt compelled to stop and give a specific word that the Lord was communicating to me. It was a number of verses from the book of Proverbs and I recited them, as I felt led to do, without additional comment:

There are six things the LORD hates, seven that are detestable to him: haughty eyes, a lying tongue, hands that shed innocent blood, a heart that devises wicked schemes, feet that are quick to rush into evil, a false witness who pours out lies and a man who stirs up dissension among brothers (Prov. 6:16–19).

The only comment I made was to add that it was my belief that, for whatever reason, it was the final phrase that the Lord wished to impress upon the congregation. I was about to resume my message when I heard the sound of sobbing emanating from several areas around the church.

I turned round to the pastor, who was sitting behind me on the platform in an attempt to elicit a clue to the scene being enacted before me. He simply sat there with a look of stunned incredulity upon his face.

I finished my message, the closing songs came to an end, but the sobbing continued. The minister drew me aside with the words, 'And so who told you about our church?' I assured him that I possessed no knowledge of either him or his congregation.

It turned out that there had been a long-running disagreement between the senior pastor and the assistant minister over the younger man's extreme position on a point of doctrine. In consequence, around twenty of the congregation had decided that they would be leaving to form a rival group within the town. While the assistant stayed at home, his followers had announced that this was to be their last meeting at the current church. It transpired that, God having intervened in the service to warn them of his disapproval of those who stir up dissension, they were the ones who had been reduced to weeping and to tears.

Perhaps the reader will infer from this that the story now comes to a happy conclusion. It's tempting to imagine alienated members running towards their wounded pastor asking for forgiveness: their sobs of remorse transformed to tears of joy as reconciliation is made and schism avoided. Not so.

The hold that the factious leader had upon those that had joined their spirit to his was so strong that even a direct word from God was unable to break it. They had been caught in a snare that carries with it such negative and destructive power that God enumerates it amongst the most heinous sins in his universe.

Rebellion is at the root of every sin. It occurred in the heavens before the creation of the world. It was the springboard from which Lucifer launched his attack upon the Trinity. It was the catalyst that brought about the fall of angels and subsequently the fall of man. It is a contagious disease that can destroy unity in a fellowship while, at the same time, its fierce fire can weld together those of a like mind.

Those who want to be free of this snare should commit themselves never to unite around a negative. I have seen people in church life who have spent years in opposition to one another find a common enemy and so become indissoluble allies. The target can be anything from people in leadership to worship style. There are few cements as strong as sedition.

When Herod saw Jesus, he was greatly pleased, because for a long time he had been wanting to see him. From what he had heard about him, he hoped to see him perform some miracle. He plied him with many questions, but Jesus gave him no answer. The chief priests and the teachers of the law were standing there, vehemently accusing him. Then Herod and his soldiers ridiculed and mocked him. Dressing him in an elegant robe, they sent him back to Pilate. *That day Herod and Pilate became friends – before this they had been enemies* (italics mine) (Lk. 23:8–12).

Relationships and prayer

I have always been challenged by the verse in Mark's Gospel that says:

Jesus entered Jerusalem and went to the temple. He looked around at everything, but since it was already late, he went out to Bethany with the Twelve (Mk. 11:11).

'What', I ask myself, 'was he looking at and what was he looking for?' I am quite sure that Jesus was not greatly interested in either the architecture or the ritual. When we read the rest of the chapter it becomes clear that he was looking for fruitfulness, faith and forgiveness – and with that I have given one of my favourite sermon outlines away!

A more compelling question is, 'When Christ stands at the door of our individual congregations, what is he looking for?' Put another way, 'What are his priorities?' If we can determine the answer to that, we have discovered the key to unlimited growth and blessing in our churches and fellowships.

When speaking at a youth retreat some time ago, a drama team decided on a poignant way to illustrate the way that we shift and reassess our priorities.

A row of chairs was placed in the centre of the room that we were invited to imagine was a boat cut adrift at sea and slowly sinking. If the status quo was maintained all lives would be lost; but if one of the occupants was to be jettisoned, there was hope that the rest may survive. It fell to the castaways to convince the audience that, whoever else was to go overboard, they at least were essential to the success of this precarious voyage. Eventually the group would vote and the die, together with the hapless loser, would be cast.

The first occupant declared an ability to navigate by the stars and pleaded to be included. The second spoke of his knowledge of survival techniques as passionately as the next declared herself to be a doctor. By the time the turn of the last individual came, few believed he would have anything significant left to contribute. The priorities had been set in most minds and it was surely this one that they would have to sacrifice. He however did not seem at all phased by the protestations of the others. When his turn came he astounded and amused everyone by announcing that there was a hole in the boat and, furthermore, he was sitting on it.

I cannot bring to mind which of them drew the short straw, but I do remember that is was not him.

How quickly our priorities change. There are times when we alter our positions because we have assimilated new data, and that is sensible and wise. On other occasions people shift direction out of fickleness.

When Paul and Barnabas healed a crippled man in Lystra the inhabitants concluded that they must be reincarnated deities and duly began to sacrifice to them. However, when the population of the city heard them protest that they were mere mortals, and encouraged them to give the glory to God, they could hardly be restrained from stoning them.[1]

The reverse scenario took place when Paul was shipwrecked on the island of Malta and the hospitable community made food for him and his fellow prisoners. Suddenly, a viper, driven out by the heat, slithers out of the conflagration and grips Paul's wrist. Those who witnessed this jumped immediately to the assumption that 'This man must be a murderer; for though he escaped from the sea, justice has not allowed him to live.' At that point, Paul shook off the viper and suffered no ill effects, leading them to conclude that he must be a god.[2]

As Jesus rode into Jerusalem on the back of a colt the crowd spread their cloaks on the road and shouted, 'Blessed is the King who comes in the name of the Lord, Peace in heaven and glory in the highest.' Before the week had come to an end the crowd were calling for his crucifixion.[3]

When I was in the United States on one occasion a friend gave me a book entitled, *The Complete Book of Church Growth*. Whilst it was impossible for any publication to live up to a title like that, it proved to be interesting reading. The author had interviewed the senior pastors of the world's largest churches and asked them to prioritise those things that they believed had been the secret of their success. In many instances the methodologies conflicted, but there were three common denominators in every congregation.

One was that in every church there was an emphasis on teaching the whole counsel of the word of God – the Scriptures being central to their faith and practice. Another was the willingness of the minister to stick with the church over the long term. In many cases the senior minister had also been the founding pastor. The third will be of no surprise – a far higher than average commitment to intercession and prayer.

If prayer is a priority with God, and we know that it is, then it follows that failure to pray hits the pause button in our churches, families and personal experience. When that occurs we have walked into a snare. Only at the point that we align our lives with his purpose and adjust our priorities to his, can we hope to hit 'fast forward'.

Given that most of us know the secret, why does praying prove to be such a struggle? One reason is that we are engaged in warfare. Another is that, though prayer has substance, it remains intangible.

In my early days as a pastor I invited a well-known Bible teacher to come and minister at my church. My temerity in asking him was only matched by his generosity in accepting. In those days John Lancaster was among my favourite preachers and remains so to this day. John was not a 'hit and run' visitor, but took time to talk and listen to what was a fledgling pastor.

Thirty years later I can still recall what went through my mind as he asked me how I was doing. I can remember thinking how much easier it must be for a bricklayer to experience job satisfaction than it was for a minister. When he came to work each day he could see the job in hand, and by the time he left at night could measure the height of the wall he had built; not so the pastor.

He had to 'believe' that the message he had preached had found its mark or the counsel that he had offered had been constructive. He has no way of 'knowing for sure' if those for whom he has a spiritual care are growing or not.

Prayer is a little like that, and that's what makes it difficult. It is because there is no way of 'feeling' that the arrow has found its mark. There is no tactile response at the end of every period of intercession.

As Daniel stood by the river Tigris after three weeks of fasting he had absolutely no way of knowing whether he had connected with God or not. Though when a powerful angel appeared he learned two tremendous truths. The first related to a prophetic scenario that was to take place and was the substance of the message. The second was a revelation that would transcend time. The angel said:

> Do not be afraid, Daniel. Since the first day that you set your mind to gain understanding and to humble yourself before your God, your words were heard, and I have come in response to them.[4]

The angel's delay had been due to a battle in the heavenlies that Daniel had been totally oblivious to. Today, with our contemporary awareness of the modern theatres of battle, we should be less surprised.

During the Gulf War, air superiority had to be guaranteed before infantry could be committed to the ground. Too often the church stands that thesis on its head. We have tended to ignore the fact that, though there is much that we can do after prayer, there is little we can accomplish before it. The only place that action comes before prayer is in the dictionary. Or, as someone has said, 'Prayer is striking the winning blow; service is gathering up the results'.

Getting to grips with this is the equivalent of taking two hands to the jaws of a metal trap and striding free, liberated to intercede.

Correctly focussed, prayer is not a 'hit and miss affair'. During 'Desert Storm' the SAS were dropped behind enemy lines with the purpose of identifying primary targets and, having done so, fixing a laser beam upon them so that aerial forces could strike them with pinpoint accuracy. When you and I are engaged in prayer, we are doing nothing less important than that. In fact, given the eternal consequences of the battle in which we fight, the importance is considerably greater.

Ed Silvoso in his book, *That None should Perish* suggests that many churches are like the Pacific fleet moored in Pearl Harbor on 7 December 1941, – sitting targets.[5] Can there be a more apt description of someone in a snare than that? He suggests that many Christians live a life more comparable to occupants of a prisoner-of-war camp than to fighting soldiers.

It matters not one jot whether you are young or old, fit or ailing, rich or poor, educated or not. Only the level of our faith limits us. In this arena of conflict, to quote S.D. Gordon, 'A person may go aside today and shut his door and as really spend an half hour in India as if he or she were there in person'.[6]

Failure to pray is sinful for a number of reasons but not least because of what it says about whom we believe is in charge of God's church.

It is sometimes only when we are faced with situations in which we are reduced to powerlessness that we eventually turn to God for help. Is it true that you pray more when you are in trouble? If it is, then you should not wonder that God allows you to occasionally experience adversity. Sometimes the only way that God can get us to our knees is to bring us to our knees or, as Abraham Lincoln once admitted, 'I have often fallen on my knees for a lack of anywhere else to go'.

There are times however when God goes deaf. I am not suggesting inadequacy in God; it is simply that he chooses not to listen to what we are saying. Two verses teach this truth: 'If I had cherished sin in my heart, the Lord would not have listened . . .' And its corollary: 'The prayer of a righteous man is powerful and effective.'[7]

In a previous book I mentioned in this context the story of Eli and Samuel.[8] It is significant that the Scriptures state at the beginning of the account, 'In those days the word of the Lord was rare; there were not many visions.' As we have seen in an earlier chapter, when the leader stalls, all who follow him are in danger of grinding to a halt. This car was most certainly parked.

Hophni and Phineas, two sons of Eli and both priests, were living way out of line. The catalogue of their crimes was extensive and, what is more, they were getting away with it. Eli had rebuked them on more than one occasion but had failed to restrain

them. He was aware that it was his responsibility to
control them or put them out of office but he
refused to do so. There were a number of reasons
for this, but the primary one was that Eli was
personally profiting from some of the scams that his
sons were involved in. There is always trouble
ahead when a prophet is out for profit. Eli was 'on
the take'.

God had spoken so often to Eli about this that it
seemed to have reached the point that whenever the
man came to seek the mind of God on behalf of the
people he would see before him an action replay of
his own disobedience. The result was inevitable. He
stopped praying.

What happens next is one of the greatest examples
of irony in the entire biblical record. The most influ-
ential leader in the land is bypassed in favour of a
small inexperienced boy whose highest pinnacle of
responsibility thus far was to have been the Temple
cleaner.

I have often wondered how Eli must have felt
when Samuel came to his room for the third time that
night and he had to tell him that, in the event that the
Lord called again, he was to say, 'Speak Lord for
your servant is listening.'

The point is often missed that the message that
Samuel eventually received was not in fact for him at
all. It was for Eli whom God had been trying to reach
for months, but was unable to because of the 'static'
of the priest's disobedience.

Now God, unable to connect, had put down the
receiver and got through on another number. God is
looking for people who are listening.

Relationship within the marriage

Perhaps one of the biggest problems in intercession is not 'unanswered prayer' but 'unheard prayer'. The Apostle Peter says that the problem sometimes arises, not from what takes place in the church, but what goes on in the home:

> Husbands, in the same way be considerate as you live with your wives, and treat them with respect as the weaker partner and as heirs with you of the gracious gift of life, so that nothing will hinder your prayers.[9]

The Amplified Bible translates the verse this way:

> In the same way you married men should live considerately with your wives with an intelligent recognition of the marriage relation, honouring the woman as physically the weaker but realizing that you are joint heirs of the grace of life; *in order that your prayers may not be hindered and cut off*. Otherwise you cannot pray effectively (italics mine).

Picture if you will a bird handler releasing a dove which, as he pulls his hands away, flutters and rises with the branches of a tall tree as its destination. Incongruous though it may appear, now imagine the same man drawing an arrow and as the bird rises, shooting it down just seconds before it lands.

Peter says that this is what happens in our prayer life when there is a dissonance between our relationship with God and the way we treat one another in the privacy of our own home. The prayer may be eloquent, biblically sound and rising with the wings of faith yet, before it reaches the throne of God, it can die by our own hands.

Keeping short accounts with God and with one another is an old recipe but it has yet to be improved upon. When the enemy of our souls sees a crack develop he has a vested interest in making it a chasm. Hence the advice that Paul gives to the Church in Ephesus.

> Each of you must put off falsehood and speak truthfully to his neighbour, for we are all members of one body. In your anger do not sin: Do not let the sun go down while you are still angry, and do not give the devil a foothold.[10]

Charlton Heston was once asked how his relationship with his wife had held together so strongly in a Hollywood culture in which so many marriages fail. His advice was simple, 'I have learned over the years the importance of those three little words . . . I was wrong!'

When we look to enhancing or repairing the relationship with our partner we are affecting far more than the small orbit of our domestic arrangements: we are directly influencing our effectiveness in the spiritual realm. Positively articulating our affirmation will make us less likely to identify with the pain of the mourning husband who, looking down on the lowered coffin was heard to say, 'She was a wonderful wife to me . . . and I nearly told her once.'

Relationship outside the marriage

We live in a Kleenex society in which relationships, tissue-paper thin, are established and abandoned with hardly a second's thought. The incidence of broken relationships within Christian homes in some areas is quickly catching up with the spiral of disintegrating commitment in secular families. Some would argue that the problems were always there and current statistics only serve to reveal a new honesty. Others, in my view nearer the truth, would suggest that the desire to work things through is not seen as a necessary building block in the society in which we live. This seems to suggest an attitude which says, 'If it's broken discard it – it's not worth the effort to mend or repair.'

Because our eyes have got used to the dark, the Church has assimilated itself chameleon-like into the secular way of thinking. Where sex is concerned, society has naively bought into the existentialist error that purports that, 'If it's not hurting anyone else then how can anything so wonderful be so wrong?' Society has taken the bait because it 'feels good', forgetting that there is always free cheese in a mouse trap. In the following passage from the book of Proverbs the seducer is the woman, though it could just as easily have been the man. Notice, once again, the fowler's snare that brings down the bird in full flight and robs it of destiny and destination:

'Come, let's drink deep of love till morning; let's enjoy ourselves with love! My husband is not at home; he

has gone on a long journey. He took his purse filled
with money and will not be home till full moon.' With
persuasive words she led him astray; she seduced him
with her smooth talk. All at once he followed her like an
ox going to the slaughter, like a deer stepping into a
noose till an arrow pierces his liver, *like a bird darting into
a snare*, little knowing it will cost him his life. Now then,
my sons, listen to me; pay attention to what I say. Do not
let your heart turn to her ways or stray into her paths.
Many are the victims she has brought down; her slain are a
mighty throng. Her house is a highway to the grave,
leading down to the chambers of death (italics mine).[11]

Many a Christian home has been plundered, not by
the wanton vamp of the book of Proverbs, but by the
'spiritual' man or woman who 'understands me
better' than my husband/wife.

Today's tendency for Christians to greet one
another with a hug, though by no means wrong in
itself, carries with it pitfalls for the vulnerable. There
can sometimes be a thin line between the embrace of
the brother and the lover.

Counselling plays a major role in many churches
and has the potential to do a great deal of good. It can
also do immeasurable damage when the compli-
cated dynamics of what psychologists term 'trans-
ference' is not taken seriously. I would suggest that
this subtle scenario has snared more high-calibre
Christians than any other ploy of the enemy. For the
sake of the illustration we will refer to the counsellor
as Joe and the client as Jane.

The presentation problem for Jane is a strained
marriage in which she perceives her husband to be

inconsiderate and lacking in affection. Joe, an experienced counsellor, listens patiently and without interruption as Jane relates her story. After a couple of sessions the first section of the snare is already open: Jane is beginning to idealise Joe. She contrasts her miserable marriage with the relaxed relationship she enjoys with her counsellor. She pictures her husband grunting over the top of his newspaper when she desperately wants to tell him about her day – and notices that Joe has not once averted his attentive gaze from her in the past thirty minutes. Could this be love? No, but if Joe is operating out of a crumbling relationship of his own and has been looking forward more than he should to this regular date in his diary, the trap has been well and truly sprung.

Perhaps you are thinking, reader, that such a thing could never happen to you. You cannot ever imagine being a Joe or a Jane. If so, read on:

> So be careful. If you are thinking, 'Oh, I would never behave like that' – let this be a warning to you. For you too may fall into sin. But remember this – the wrong desires that come into your life aren't anything new and different. Many others have faced exactly the same problems before you. And no temptation is irresistible. You can trust God to keep the temptation from becoming so strong that you can't stand up against it, for he has promised this and will do what he says. He will show you how to escape temptation's power so that you can bear up patiently against it.[12]

There are no arguments here against genuine warmth between fellow-Christians or of removing counselling from the curriculum of the church. In the same way that one would not advocate the removal of pedestrians from the road lest a car hit them, one might proffer the advice that they confine themselves to the pavements.

Relationships and forgiveness

I have discovered that the summoning and subsequent arrival of a recovery vehicle evokes a myriad of mixed emotions. The anxiety of the breakdown moves into an emerging relief when you are told that help is on its way and, as you see it appear over the horizon, there is hope that the whole irritable interlude will soon be over. The request to open the bonnet brings a sense of confidence that a professional is at work as he prods and pokes around the perimeter of the engine. It is at this point that a measured sense of apprehension begins to rear its head. What brings it on is the peculiar sound that most mechanics make at this juncture. It consists of a sharp intake of breath accompanied usually by the slow shaking of the head. This in my experience is meant to convey the idea that this is a bigger problem than first thought and I am driven further to the conclusion that each intake of break represents around £50. In short, the knowledge that you are immobilised changes to relief that help is imminent but reverts to disquiet when you realize that continuing your journey will involve a price to be paid.

I know of very few people who would abandon their vehicle because they were unwilling to face the cost of repair. I have encountered in my time, however, many Christians whose progress has come to a standstill, who sit stalled in a lay-by as they haggle with God about the price exacted by repentance. The restorer of souls has come alongside and challenged them to 'open up'. They may have done so for a time but, when the cost of resuming their journey is discovered, they slam the bonnet shut, their destiny and destination abandoned.

This is never more graphically illustrated than in the person who possesses a spirit of unforgiveness.

Evangelicals identify keenly with the truth that the grace of God is greater than our sin. Our reflexes instinctively recoil from the Roman Catholic concept of penance. We proudly proclaim that grace is free and that salvation is not of works. 'All that is needed' we cry with the conviction of Luther nailing his thesis on the doors of Wittenberg Cathedral, 'is a repentant heart and God will do the rest.'

Well, grace is certainly free and repentance a requirement but, as for God doing the rest – if only it were always as easy as that.

A person may be truly sorry for their sin against another, and run to God in repentance as their sole resource, but if they are not willing to forgive those who have sinned against them, the exercise may distance them from the full resource of God's grace for them.

Jesus said, 'For if you forgive men when they sin against you, your heavenly Father will also forgive you.

But if you do not forgive men their sins, your Father will not forgive your sins.'[13]

The opportunity to repair relationships is offered to us each time we remember the cross at the communion service and we do well to take seriously the verses that say:

> Whoever eats the bread or drinks the cup of the Lord in an unworthy manner will be guilty of sinning against the body and blood of the Lord. A man ought to examine himself before he eats of the bread and drinks of the cup. For anyone who eats and drinks without recognising the body of the Lord eats and drinks judgement on himself. That is why many among you are weak and sick, and a number of you have fallen asleep. But if we judge ourselves, we would not come under judgement. When we are judged by the Lord, we are being disciplined so that we will not be condemned with the world.[14]

This is interpreted by many to mean that if they are not in good relationship with others then they should let the communion emblems pass by when they are offered. This may even be accompanied by a warm glow of personal satisfaction that they have taken the matter seriously enough to make such a gesture. The fact is that there is no scriptural sanction for doing this. The exhortation is to examine ourselves before eating. In other words, the assumption is that if the Holy Spirit has highlighted in us the need to repair a relationship, then we commit ourselves to doing this at our earliest opportunity. This then makes it possible for us to partake. This passage does not give us a mandate to live in perpetual disobedience to God by harbouring an attitude of unforgiveness.

'But', I hear someone say, 'I am the wounded party, it is not my place to make the first move. They have wronged me and it is they who should instigate reconciliation.'

The Bible assumes that if you are the one sinned against you are in a more spiritual place than the 'sinner' and therefore more likely to respond to the promptings of God and repair the relationship.

> Therefore, if you are offering your gift at the altar and there remember that your brother has something against you, leave your gift there in front of the altar. First go and be reconciled to your brother; then come and offer your gift.[15]

I have always been challenged by the statement, 'The Lord Jesus, on the night he was betrayed, took bread'. By leaving us this example he shows us both the perils of this pernicious snare and the way out of it.

It is said that on one occasion Leonardo da Vinci was painting a picture that centred around the face of Jesus, when a group of small boys came to his studio to visit him. He was annoyed that his concentration had been broken, but became especially angry when one of them knocked over a large stack of canvasses. Incensed, the artist threw his brush and a few harsh words at the little fellow who ran crying from the apartment. Glad that they were gone he attempted to resume his work but, try as he might, he found it impossible to continue. Eventually, putting down his palate, he went outside and roamed the streets until he had found the boy concerned and, having apologised for his anger, returned home. He was then able to finish the masterpiece that has since been an inspiration to millions.

It was C.S. Lewis who said, 'We all believe that forgiveness is a beautiful idea until we have to practise it ourselves. To be a Christian means to forgive the inexcusable because God has forgiven the inexcusable in you.'

This brings us to a place of necessary brokenness. Our reflex reaction is to discard broken things. With God brokenness is a prerequisite of acceptance. Peter was impetuous and the proud possessor of a good deal of natural self-confidence. It is he who walked on the water when others shivered in the boat. It is Peter who promises never to forsake his Lord but then fails so spectacularly. Yet it was not until he had 'gone out and wept bitterly', and the scaffolding of self-assurance began to be dismantled, that he became vulnerable enough for God to use him. Three thousand souls saved on the day of Pentecost came through the preaching of a man who was emptied of himself in order that he might be filled with the Holy Spirit.

The Tongue Trap

A fool's mouth is his undoing, and his lips are a snare to his soul (Prov. 18:7).

The book of Psalms is the Christian on his knees and the book of Proverbs is the Christian on his feet. Proverbs give motion to devotion.

When reading Proverbs I have sometimes found it helpful to take a subject, such as evangelism for example, and then to read the book noting as I go along all the verses that are applicable to it. When an exercise such as this is done on 'the tongue' the data retrieved is intriguing.

In the New Testament it is James who points us to the sharpest definition of the tongue's destructive potential:

When we put bits into the mouths of horses to make them obey us, we can turn the whole animal. Or take ships as an example. Although they are so large and are driven by strong winds, they are steered by a very small rudder wherever the pilot wants to go. Likewise the tongue is a small part of the body, but it makes great boasts. Consider what a great forest is set on fire by a small spark. The tongue also is a fire, a world of evil among the parts of the body. It corrupts the whole person, sets the whole course of his life on fire, and is itself set on fire by hell.[1]

When it comes to the many snares from which the believer needs to be extricated, it may be thought that the mouth trap should be relegated to the bottom of the list. Yet it is this 'small rudder' that has steered innumerable ships from their charted course to shipwreck on the rocks of verbal indiscretion. How many of us would have wished that we could take back things that we have said perhaps milliseconds after they have been uttered? In many cases the damage done will have been slight, in some instances irreparable.

Criticism

There is of course positive criticism. Most of us welcome it as a way of building us up and helping us to gather a wider perspective. We know the reality of the truth that 'Wounds from a friend can be trusted'.[2] There is no snare there, only emancipation.

Bill Hybels, Senior Pastor of Willow Creek Community Church in Chicago, believes that when conflict goes underground it poisons the soil. In replying to critical letters he begins by saying, 'Thank you so much for the courage it took to express your displeasure with me. I don't take lightly your willingness to follow the biblical injunction to come direct to me.' He adds, 'When you swim in the ocean you get attacked by sharks and guppies – don't worry about the guppies.'

Negative criticism however can be devastating in its savagery. The child's retort in the playground that 'Sticks and stones may break my bones but names will never hurt me' may be bathed in bravado but for many it simply is not true.

> The mouth of the righteous is a fountain of life, but violence overwhelms the mouth of the wicked.[3]

Much has been written about negative words spoken over the young and impressionable. It was not Freud who first discovered the fact that things inscribed on the soft tablet of a child's heart become cemented into later life and that the heat of experience bakes it harder still.

The counselling rooms of pastors are full of those who are physically mature and strong but have an 'inner child' that has unhealed wounds. Thank God it *is* possible to escape this snare but only with a willingness to believe what God is saying; rather than what others have stamped into you.

Two verses tucked away in 1 Chronicles give us an insight into both the nature of the manacle and its key. They tell the story of a woman carrying a child, with all the anticipation that a promised birth brings. The delivery however proves to be horrendous and the woman suffers greatly.

She decides that the boy born to her should carry the burden of the suffering he has caused for as long as he lives. She names him 'pain-bringer'. His earliest memory of being called to his mother's side reinforces that he was, and perhaps always will be, a troublemaker. At every introduction he has to endure the stigma of someone who has a 'past'. No new relationships are ever forged without the burden of a name from yesterday that advertises him as someone to be wary of. As he grows into manhood, he manages against all the odds to build a reputation of his own, so much so that within his family he outshines those siblings that do not have to carry his terrible tag.

Yet, despite every effort on his part, he still finds his horizons narrowed. He is snared by a signature that his parents have written across his future as defacing as if it had been graffiti scrawled across a work of art. That is what censure does. However beautiful the masterpiece, there is something perverse about human nature in that it is more willing to examine the superficial than investigate the substance beneath. He realizes that he does not have a social or psychological problem but that what had happened has become so ingrained that only God can bring about his restoration. The day he cries out to God, in a mixture of faith and desperation, the snare inside him snaps. He is free. New vistas are opened before him. Fresh, attainable horizons beckon him forward.

Jabez was more honourable than his brothers. His mother had named him Jabez, saying, 'I gave birth to him in pain'. Jabez cried out to the God of Israel, 'Oh, that you would bless me and enlarge my territory! Let your hand be with me, and keep me from harm so that I will be free from pain'. And God granted his request.[4]

Perhaps you are reading this and recognize a mirrored reflection of your own experience. It may be that your early years are remembered as a time when, hard as you tried, you could never attain your parents' approval. If there were brothers or sisters who were preferred to you, or you endured a childhood in which there was an absence of love, you will be able to understand Jabez better than most.

The important thing is to recognise that there is a way out. You are not stuck in the sidings like an abandoned railway carriage. The points are changing and rescue is on the way. Let faith and desperation rise in you. Break out. Break free. Move on.

Those who tentatively launch out into new areas can find their vessel quickly waterlogged by the thoughtless faultfinder. I have encountered people who find it hard to pray in public because their first attempts were berated by some sour soul who suggested ways in which they would have done it better. It has always been my view that no one should criticize another unless they are distinguishing themselves by their own performance. A person busy pulling on the oars has little time to rock the boat.

When a famous evangelist, who had led multitudes to Christ, was accosted by a man who said that he was not too happy about the preacher's style, the evangelist asked his accuser how many people he had brought to the Lord. When the man admitted that he had never seen anyone come to faith, the evangelist replied that he preferred his way of doing it to his critic's way of not doing it.

When a young musician was disheartened by the review his first concert had received in the press, the famous Finnish composer Jean Sibelius consoled him by saying, 'Remember, son, there is no city in the world where they have erected a statue to a critic.'

There are times when those who have been quick to point out the faults of others find themselves hoist by their own petard when they are catapulted into the situation themselves. When a lady, known for her comments on her husband's driving style, found herself stalled and causing a traffic jam, she turned to him in desperation asking what she should do next. His reply was, 'I don't know but I'm sure that you will be able to figure it out as soon as you climb into the back seat.' Lest I disengage from all my women readers at this point, let me point out that it is not just one sex that has the monopoly on carping criticism. It's always easier to fix the blame than fix the problem.

The fact is that those who engage in these forms of verbal vandalism seem totally inured, not only to the damage that they can cause, but also to any present pain that their victim was enduring before their attack was launched.

In 1992 a Los Angeles policeman came across a Brown Cadillac that was illegally parked. The policeman dutifully placed a $30 ticket on the screen and, as the driver made no argument, the police officer drove away. What the policeman had failed to observe was that the driver was dead. He had been shot through the head several times more than twelve hours before. The policeman had been so engrossed in ticket writing, he had not noticed.

The callous critic all too easily slaps their verbal 'fines' on the windscreens of the wounded, insensitive to their current situation.

It was Theodore Roosevelt who said, 'It is not the critic who counts; not the man who points out how the strong man stumbles, or where the doer of deeds could have done them better. The credit belongs to the man who is actually in the arena, whose face is marred by dust and sweat and blood; who strives valiantly, who errs and comes short again and again, because there is no effort without error and shortcomings . . . at worst, if he fails, at least he fails while daring greatly, so that his place shall never be with those cold and timid souls who know neither victory nor defeat.'

Reckless words pierce like a sword, but the tongue of the wise brings healing.[5]

Gossip

If there is anything worse than the destructive critic it is the gossip. Though we know they abound, they are the most illusive of creatures. I have never yet met anyone who has admitted to possessing this propensity. Gossip is always something that someone else does. Some seek to sanitise it with the argument that real gossips are those who pass on untrue and scurrilous stories. The fact is that gossips will never tell a lie if the truth will do as much damage. As William Blake put it, 'A truth that is told with bad intent beats all the lies you can invent.'

Others spiritualize it. They will never say, 'I heard Joe and Mary's marriage is in real trouble.' They will say, 'I think we should pray about Joe and Mary, I've heard their marriage is in real trouble.'

The church that does not get to grips with gossip will never hope to see the blessing of God upon it. It is a deadly and cancerous disease. Yet how many churches would remove from membership those who perpetrate it? They indulge in selective sanctification. Their members grumble, gossip and criticize with impunity but are never disciplined because they have never been guilty of 'real sins' like smoking and drinking. The Bible says:

> A gossip betrays a confidence, so avoid a man who talks too much.[6]

Anger

Relationships can take years to build and seconds to destroy. One sentence uttered in anger can undo a lifetime's work. Even when reconciliation is realized, cutting remarks are remembered for a long time afterwards. They stay like heat stains on a shiny surface – you can polish over them but their ghostly presence still remains, however much time may try to fade them.

> Better a patient man than a warrior, a man who controls his temper than one who takes a city.[7]

The idle word

The King James Version calls them 'idle words,' though the NIV refers to them as 'careless'. Jesus said:

> I tell you that men will have to give account on the day of judgement for every careless word they have spoken. For by your words you will be acquitted, and by your words you will be condemned.[8]

An idle word is like an idle person. It is a word that does not work. The unfulfilled promise, especially when uttered to God, is a trap for the soul. God takes the vows we make to him seriously. We expect our heavenly father to stand by his word and he expects us, as his children to display the same family trait. The idle word is the sin for which Ananias and Sapphira[9] were judged and subsequently received capital punishment. They died, not because they did not give the entire proceeds of their land to God, but because they promised to give the entire proceeds of their land to God and failed to do so.

On one occasion I was speaking at a youth event at which there were around two thousand teenagers present. At the close of the message I made an appeal for reconsecration and there was a large response. Normally I would find such a moment moving. On this evening however, as young men and women made their way from the balconies and floor of the building to the front, I was aware of a sense of heaviness. I had made the call clear. It had not been a vague, bland or emotional appeal; but I still felt burdened.

I was heavy in spirit because I could not help but wonder how many of those who crowded the altar would forget the commitment they were making before the coach in which they had come had stopped at the first motorway service station on the way home. I wondered, because I knew that there had been times in my life when I had done the same thing, promised everything and produced so very little in comparison with the weight of my words.

I thought, as I made my own way home, of the time when God had made a covenant with Abraham, and all that Abraham was called to do was to provide the sacrifice, place it on the ground, and God would do the rest. As he did so, something sinister yet significant took place. The birds of the air flew down to devour the sacrifice before God had uttered a word.[10] The Bible says that Abraham's reaction was to drive the birds away with his staff.

Oh that we all had such reflex obedience and refused to allow the 'prince of the power of the air' to devour our commitment before we had time to place it before God.

The idle word is a snare to the soul because it does not allow our emotion to metamorphose from the chrysalis of consecration into the butterfly of action. Instead it lies immobile on the ground and vulnerable to any passing predator. When this takes place faith, being without works, has died.

It is not only at the point of prayer that a person is snared by words of unfulfilled promise. It happens more often than we dare imagine during times of praise and worship.

A friend of mine recounted the story of when he was the guest speaker at a local church. The format of the service was typical of a charismatic gathering – a period of praise prior to the moment he would be invited to bring the message. He looked down at the stack of overheads that were placed at the side of the projector and watched as one by one the pile was reduced in size.

The quality of the music was as excellent as the enthusiasm of the congregation was unbounded. Yet he was becoming increasingly disturbed in his spirit. As the current song was in mid-flight he slowly walked over to the projector and switched it off. One can only imagine the effect that this must have had on the congregation. The singing ground to a halt as did the music. He approached the microphone and softly asked how many people could recall the song before last. No one raised their hand. He selected the appropriate transparency from its out-tray and, switching on the projector, displayed it. The theme of the song was total surrender. It had been offered to God only minutes earlier and no one could even remember singing it! The message he conveyed by that act might well have been a more eloquent sermon than any exposition that was to follow. You may conclude that my friend was harsh. I have come to the conclusion that, though we may dismiss the sentiments that we sing and promises we pray, I am not entirely sure that God does.

Do not be quick with your mouth, do not be hasty in your heart to utter anything before God. God is in heaven and you are on earth, so let your words be few. As a dream comes when there are many cares, so the speech of a fool when there are many words. When you make a vow to God, do not delay in fulfilling it. He has no pleasure in fools; fulfil your vow. It is better not to vow than to make a vow and not fulfil it. Do not let your mouth lead you into sin.[11]

The idle word of 'prophecy'

I want to say at the outset that I believe in prophecy, both in its forth telling and foretelling contexts. I believe in words for the gathered church and the individual and when I minister, subsequent to an altar call, that may well be part of a ministry that I would exercise. I would also add that I believe that the vast majority of words of revelation that are given are ministered out of a basis of integrity and anointing.

Having made this point, I am increasingly disturbed about the 'fake fire' that accompanies some itinerant ministries that blow in, blow up and blow out – leaving local leaders to deal with lives that have been damaged as a result.

I was preaching at an inter-church celebration some time ago and felt led to make an appeal that related to this subject. I inquired if there were any in the congregation that considered themselves trapped by a word that had been spoken over their life that they had now come to feel was not from God.

When people were asked to come forward, they approached the front of the auditorium in their scores. Two weeks earlier I had made a similar appeal at a Bible week in Wales and the results had been the same – dozens snared in a vortex of what can only be described as spiritual abuse. In many cases they were vulnerable people who had been sincerely seeking for answers. They had been looking for bread and had been offered a stone.

Some had been promised an international ministry that was 'just around the corner' and were living their lives on 'hold' in anticipation of that door being opened. Another couple, desperate for children, had been told they would definitely have a baby in their arms within the year. Years had passed, as had a hysterectomy, and they were still 'holding on to God' for the fulfilment of a promise that he had never made.

A pastor recently told me about a man who had spoken at his church and told a young woman who had come out for ministry that, 'She should not worry as the baby would arrive soon.' This woman was not married nor was she even in a relationship. She left the church embarrassed and publicly humiliated.

God will not have his word or his children handled in such a way. Under the old covenant the penalty for such sin was death. I cannot believe that God will compromise his prophetic standards under the new dispensation.

A prophet who presumes to speak in my name anything I have not commanded him to say, or a prophet who speaks in the name of other gods, must be put to

death. You may say to yourselves, 'How can we know
when a message has not been spoken by the Lord?' If
what a prophet proclaims in the name of the Lord does
not take place or come true, that is a message the Lord
has not spoken. That prophet has spoken presumptu-
ously. Do not be afraid of him.[12]

This is a snare that not only holds people back from
God's real purpose for them but, when it fails, has
the perverse effect of causing them to doubt anyone
who brings them a word from God however genuine
it may be. They have been doubly trapped.

'How can we know?' was the question posed in
the book of Deuteronomy. We will look at some tests
for 'weighing' words.

Look at the prophet

What do you know about this man or woman? Do
they have credibility with you? I did not ask if they
were famous or popular – that is a different question.
Do you know them to be living under the spiritual
authority of someone to whom they are accountable?
If they were to 'get it wrong' are they accessible
enough for you to contact them?

Look at the motive

Prophecies and 'words' can be extremely manipula-
tive. Those who purport to exercise the gift hold
immense power over someone who is looking for an
anointed word from the Lord and for guidance in
their life.

I was speaking at a conference on one occasion and met a member of a church I had once pastored. This man was a commodities broker and I had always considered him and his family to be stable and sensible people. When I inquired about one of his daughters he told me the following story.

She and her husband had been told by an internationally-known faith teacher to give up their careers, sell their home, fly to a certain international airport on the other side of the world and wait until a messenger from the Lord came to tell them the next step. They did everything as instructed.

When no one met them at the airport terminal, all that they had believed in instantly dissolved at their feet and they resolved never to have anything to do with the things of God again. He had let them down. God had failed them. The truth of the matter was that God had nothing at all to do with the issue. They had fallen into a satanic snare that had been set by an angel of light.

I can almost hear the reader gasp with incredulity at the apparent naivety of a person who would respond to a 'word' in such a way. Yet one would have to understand that this preacher's videos, tapes and books had been their meat and drink for years. His 'word' had pressed a button in them for he was speaking of a future destiny that they dreamed of for themselves. This man was not wrong because he was a faith teacher: he was wrong because he was wrong. His controlling influence was too seductive to resist.

Then the Lord said to me, 'The prophets are prophesying lies in my name. I have not sent them or appointed

them or spoken to them. They are prophesying to you
false visions, divinations, idolatries and the delusions
of their own minds.'[13]

Look at the prophecy

No one should ever make a move on the basis of a
predictive prophecy until they know it to be the
confirmation of a word that God had placed in their
heart over a protracted period of time. I am speaking
of more than a long-held aspiration that they may
have had. It is all too easy to project dreams on to
fleeces.

Have you ever noticed that if you are thinking of
buying a certain make of car the motorways seem to
be filled with that precise model? It is not that they
have suddenly appeared for your benefit or that
guidance is involved. It is simply that the vehicle has
been uppermost in your mind and you are 'seeing
them' everywhere you go.

If someone, whom I had never previously met,
came and told me that God wants me to sell all and
move to India, the chances of me packing my bags
are remote. If on the other hand I had felt burdened
for that continent for a long period, and was looking
for confirmation of the right timing to move, then I
would consider the word very seriously indeed.

Before we conclude this section let me say something about the 'writing down' of prophetic words. It
is my view that any word given should be recorded
so that you can weigh it thoroughly and pray it
through. There are two provisos however that
should be kept firmly in mind.

The first is that the prophecy should be held in correct 'proportion' to biblical revelation: some people carry 'words' at the back of their Bibles as if they were an addendum to the Scriptures, which they are not.

The second proviso, and this is particularly important when we consider 'foretelling' prophecy, is that it should be retained in a chronological context. A word given to you three years ago may not be pertinent to the spiritual condition you are in today. The word was right for then but not for now. To act on it then would be helpful, to act on it today may be harmful. Let me illustrate.

Imagine for a moment I have arrived at your church car park and am having some difficulty reversing into a parking space. You are kind enough to offer me assistance and your guidance consists of . . . right, right, left hand down, straight back. You have helped me and I am grateful. If however I write those instructions down, and keep them for the next time I need to park, then I am likely to do serious damage to adjacent cars. Why? Because on this occasion I am 'starting from a different place'.

I feel that in some churches there needs to be a moratorium on 'words' until fulfilment catches up with prediction. When too much money is in circulation the value of the currency tumbles. When too many 'words' are in circulation the credibility of prophecy falls.

5

Small Ambition

Why do some churches remain small? How can it be that through successive generations congregations do not grow in size – even though they are surrounded by multitudes of people? Can such churches break out of the shackles of smallness or are they to be consigned forever to their dungeon of diminutive expectation? I am convinced that one of the primary reasons why fellowships fail to grow is because of the way they perceive themselves and their future. Before we address this vital issue we will highlight other reasons that, in a minority of cases, may also be a contributing factor.

A bad birth

As we have seen in a previous chapter, if a church is formed out of schism, its foundations are as shallow as its destiny is limited. To escape the snare the current leadership, whether personally culpable or not, needs to make contact with the branch from which they were severed and seek genuine reconciliation. A letter, or chat over coffee, will not usually suffice. Something needs to be broken in the heavenlies so that the spiritual constraints can be removed. In some cases the group may need to return. In others, financial 'fruits of repentance' need to be returned. In every case serious sorrow for sin needs to be shown and a heart to 'work together in the future' exhibited. Failure to do so will incarcerate them in a snare that has been set by Satan himself.

> '. . . in the hope that God will grant them repentance leading them to a knowledge of the truth, and that they will come to their senses and escape from the trap of the devil, who has taken them captive to do his will'. (2 Timothy 2:25–26)

Clearly there are some occasions when it has been right and necessary for a group to move away. The fact is that there has never been a split where the out-going party has felt unjustified in its actions. The plain truth is that some were right and some were wrong. Where the reasons were spiritually unsupportable, a snare has been set and, though they pray for blessing to the point of exhaustion, nothing will progress until reality is faced and the hindrance to growth and blessing removed.

Poor leadership

There is a sense in which I am somewhat reticent to approach this section. This is not because, being a

minister myself, I want to engage in over-protective-
ness for the people for whom I have a high regard
and am numbered amongst. Neither is it because
pastors are beyond reproach. It is due to the fact that
I am aware of a propensity amongst some church
members to deflect responsibility away from themselves and set leadership up as a perpetual scapegoat
for the demise of their church.

I was once approached by a lady who set about
criticizing our youth leader on the basis that her
teenage son was in a backslidden state. 'How could
the church allow my child to get into such a
position?' she remonstrated. 'How can that man call
himself a leader?' I knew this woman well. I was also
aware that she and her husband were arch critics of
the direction that the church was heading and was
never reluctant to share her opinions with anyone
who would give her an ear.

The leader was a fine man and working hard to
create a programme for growth and wholeness
amongst our young people. I endeavoured to point
out to her that her boy was under the influence of the
church for a few hours a week but lived in her home
twenty-four hours a day. If influence was the issue,
who should shoulder the greatest responsibility for
the state her child was in? What I really wanted to
say to her was, 'If your child is continually breathing
in a polluted atmosphere of criticism and gossip in
the home, you should not be greatly surprised that
he has developed into a spiritual asthmatic.'

This having been said, there clearly is a responsibility on the pastor and, as we shall see later, the
eldership to create a framework for spiritual growth

within the church. If the leadership has become a prisoner of any of the snares outlined in the first chapter, they will need to deal with that. If, for example, the pastor is not giving attention to the ministry of the word in preparation and prayer, then the congregation will become emaciated and weak. God's people have not been born into the Kingdom to live on fast food.

It is even possible that the leader may not have been called by God in the first place. If this is the situation, for the sake of the church, himself and his family, that reality needs to be faced.

Those that lead, alongside the pastor, have the potential to be a barrier or a blessing – a help or a hindrance. During my ministry I have been conscious of being fortunate in the calibre of leaders that God has placed alongside me. In every fellowship I have pastored I have worked with those who were able to marry gifting and vision with a servant heart. I am also acutely aware that there are many congregations where this is by no means the case.

In some churches, leaders are in place only because they have more family in the congregation than anyone else and have been voted into position solely on that basis. They see themselves as 'office bearers' and this can be clearly seen in the way they conduct themselves. They appear unaware that God is more concerned with function than with office. Their role is a power-base from which to operate rather than an opportunity to serve. As Chuck Swindol has pointed out, when alluding to Jesus washing the disciples' feet, 'People are far more willing to fight over thrones than towels.'

If this were a book solely on the subject of the nature of the Church in a new millennium, we would need also to address the importance of team, salaried or not, and the development of the five-fold ministries. This however is not the primary purpose before us.

Democratisation

The Bible gives two reasons why a person should think twice about becoming a spiritual leader.[1] The first is that they are going to be judged more severely than those they are leading. The second is that leaders, apart from giving an answer for the way in which they have conducted their lives as individuals, will also be required to answer for the lives of all those that God has placed under their care.

> Obey your leaders and submit to their authority. They keep watch over you as men who must give an account. Obey them so that their work will be a joy, not a burden, for that would be of no advantage to you (Heb. 13:17).

Leaders themselves must also be accountable to those who are in authority over them, otherwise they have no right to exercise authority over others. There are no lone-rangers in God's economy.

In some churches this principle is turned on its head to such a degree that, rather than the shepherd leading the sheep, the sheep are perpetually telling the shepherd what to do. I have seen pastors who are like stray dogs at a whistler's convention – running around furiously in a vain attempt to accommodate everybody's whim and keep everybody happy.

This is not to say that pastors should not solicit the views of those they lead. Church government should be as open and transparent as possible. Leaders should continually bring before the people in their charge the vision that God has put on their heart and, when appropriate, inquire as to whether it has their assent. This however is a far cry from leadership asking permission to alter every clause and comma in a constitution. In some fellowships, commas have driven the church into comas.

I have witnessed the snare that traps the individual. I have seen snares that capture a church. On one occasion democracy was a snare that imprisoned an entire nation.

Moses had brought the Children of Israel to the very borders of the land that God had promised them and, operating on his instruction, Moses sent out spies to investigate it (Num. 13,14). When the committee reported back, two said they should advance and ten said they should retreat. Democracy prevailed and, tethered to their snare, over two million people wandered around in circles for forty years.

The names of Shammua, Shaphat, Igal, Palti, Gaddiel, Gaddi, Ammiel, Sethur, Nahbi, Geuel, are enshrined forever in the minutes of Scripture as the men who 'won the vote'. Perhaps they went home to their wives proud that they had out-manoeuvred the dark forces of radicalism. It may be that Caleb and Joshua left the leadership meeting wondering if it was worth staying on. The vote may have been won but the day had been lost. It is possible to win a ballot and loose a battle and, proud though these men may have been in the short term, it is not for winning they are remembered. They are known now only for their faithlessness.

The heroes are Joshua and Caleb: people who stayed in their place despite democratic reversal. The saddest part of this story is that lack of faith not only snared the pessimists, it made captives of those who had a heart to 'move on'.

The writer of the book of Hebrews looks back on that dreadful day in this way:

> The message they heard was of no value to them, because those who heard it did not combine it with faith.[2]

It may be that, like me, you have witnessed an animal released from a trap and have watched it race to the freedom of the open countryside, putting as much distance as it can between its captors and itself. I feel I am a spectator at such a scene when I look at the life of Caleb – a man of a 'different spirit'. I could easily append the relevant text to the appendix, but I want you to read it for yourself. I want it to do you good. It may be that your relationship to someone, via marriage or church affiliation, has meant that because others have wandered into a snare and you are joined to them, you are equally imprisoned. These verses show that however old you are and however long it's been, it's never too late to let faith give you wings. It is the story of an eighty-five year old man.

Now then, just as the Lord promised, he has kept me alive for forty-five years since the time he said this to Moses, while Israel moved about in the desert. So here I am today, eighty-five years old! I am still as strong today as the day Moses sent me out; I'm just as vigorous to go out to battle now as I was then. Now give me this hill country that the Lord promised me that day. You yourself heard then that the Anakites were there and their cities were large and fortified, but, the Lord helping me, I will drive them out just as he said.[3]

Isn't that wonderful? That account is all about vision and breaking free from the restrictions placed upon us by others or by adverse circumstances. I would ask you to pause at this point in your reading. Put this book to one side and agree with me that, whatever it is that you identify as holding you back today, God has the power to release you in the area of your spirit. Be a caged bird no more. Allow the bars to fall away. You are free to soar.

The favour of God

Destiny is not chance but choice. It is a synthesis of God's choices and ours; of his sovereignty and our responsibility.

Every powerful and successful ministry began with small choices. It may have demanded major steps of faith as it developed but, before it hit the headlines, someone somewhere took the first initial small step of obedience. Huge doors hang on small hinges. Some of the choices you will make today may have significant long-term consequences for yourself and your family. If you are married, think of those two words you spoke at the altar, 'I do', and consider where they have led you.

God is asking you not to despise the day of small things. It is what you do with what you've got that will determine what you get tomorrow. That is what the parable of the talents is all about.

I have pastored churches large and small. As mentioned earlier in the book, a number of these fellowships began with just a small handful of people. It usually took a year before the small cell had grown to the place where it could begin to support a pastor of its own. When that watershed was reached I would put in place a leader and then move on to the next opportunity.

In every case I told the embryonic congregations that, when they were asked about the size of the church they attended, they were not to describe it as a 'small church'. They were always to say, 'a small church at the moment'. I wanted the anticipation of growth to be built right into the foundations. What the people believed themselves to be today would have a profound effect on what they would become tomorrow.

Reader, I want you to know that God has only got good plans for you. He does not have one poor purpose for your life. The Devil has got more dark plots than you would ever want to know about but, 'Greater is he that is in you than he that is in the world'. Expect God to favour you. It is part of your inheritance as a child of the King.

'God has no favourites!' I wonder how many times that has been said by preachers and people alike when they hear of revivals across the globe, blazing free like wild-fire. It is almost as if the Great Sower, instead of seed, were broadcasting live coals from his basket and letting them cascade across his Kingdom causing powerful conflagrations wherever they fall.[4]

He does not love Pensacola more than Pakistan or Korea more than Karachi. Yet, while God does not show favouritism, not everyone experiences his favour to the same degree.

God never shows favouritism in the realm of justice. When Peter experienced his rooftop trance and, in the vision, refused food that had previously been forbidden by Old Testament law, he knew that God had more than just his diet in mind. A cry from the gate roused him and, climbing down from his elevated position like a chastened Zacchaeus, he hurtled into a whole new world of God's revelatory purpose. The eventual object of it all was not just Cornelius but you and me – the Gentile world. Salvation was an option, not just for the Jew, but for all that would believe. 'I now realize', he declares, 'how true it is that God does not show favouritism'. Paul, in his letter to the Romans, also concluded that God does not discriminate on racial grounds any more than, as he explained to the Ephesians, he shows favouritism on the basis of culture or class. In other words, as the Colossians were told, 'Anyone who does wrong will be repaid for his wrong, and there is no favouritism.'

70 12 3 1

Yet God does discriminate in the sphere of blessing.

Jesus sent out the seventy but it was the twelve that remained closest to him. Within that group he had the inner circle of Peter, James and John. It would have seemed to the others that these three owned a season ticket to privilege. At the Transfiguration, at the raising of Jairus' daughter – even at Gethsemane it was this trio that occupied the front seats. Even amongst them John was considered the closest to Jesus.

Did the seventy have a problem with the twelve or the twelve with the three or the three with the one? When the challenge did raise its head on one occasion the Messiah's response was, 'What is that to you?' He was making it clear that he alone was the sole arbiter of where his favour rests.

Most of us long to live in the sunshine of God's favour. The reflex reaction of those of us who have visited the scenes of contemporary revival around the world is, 'Lord do not pass us by . . . may our land also know your touch.'

Sovereignty and favour

Why Mary? Why should this young woman be the one chosen from among millions to bring the Christ-child into the world? There is no logical reason that can be comprehended by the finite human mind. God had made a decision and that was that. All the angel was willing to offer by way of explanation was, 'Do not be afraid Mary, you have found favour with God.'

'Found favour'? Does this mean that she had been searching for it? There is no question that, even in her wildest dreams, she would have contemplated the possibility that she would be the one that would give birth to God's Messiah. This young woman already had a heart for God. God's choices are not capricious nor are they random and indiscriminate. There was purpose in the heavens and there still is.

It is at this point that those who hunger for God's favour to rest on their lives, their families and their churches, begin to discover the warm glow of hope. For, while God is sovereign and acts according to his own purpose, there are ways in which we can position ourselves to be in a place to receive the favour that God desires should be ours.

Right at the beginning of time God looked in favour upon Abel because of his obedience. Two chapters later in Genesis we read that Noah, 'found favour in the eyes of the Lord'. Nehemiah expected that his devotion to God would attract his favour and Moses actively sought it.

Nor is experiencing God's favour a static experience. Of Samuel the Bible says, 'The boy continued to grow in stature and in favour with the Lord'.

Almost nothing on earth is as potent as the coming together of those two powerful ingredients: the sovereignty of God and a heart that is set to please him. 'If my people who are called by my name will humble themselves and pray and seek my face and turn from their wicked ways, then will I hear from heaven and will forgive their sin and heal their land.'

The evidence of favour

What do we really mean by 'favour'? I have discovered that the Bible highlights seven distinct aspects to it.

1. An increased consciousness of God's presence	Ex. 33:13,14
2. A knowledge of the peace of God	Lk. 2:14
3. Fruitfulness	Lev. 26:8,9
4. People of destiny	Deut. 33:23
5. Experiencing blessing	Deut. 33:23
6. Having the ear of God	2 Kgs. 13:4
7. A sense of security	Ps. 5:12

Loss of favour

Some live in a sense of God's favour and then, for whatever reason, seem to slip away from it. At that point one, or all, of the above factors not only seem to be absent but, on some occasions, reversed. The problem may be nothing other than a period of spiritual struggle in which the enemy of our soul seeks to live up to his name as a devourer and a destroyer. On other occasions it might occur through our disobedience or a shifting of priorities in which Christ is moved from his central position of Lordship and is subordinated to the margins of the heart.

Some years ago Jim Bakker, who was considered a star amongst television evangelists, crashed to earth. The scandals that surrounded his demise rocked the entire Christian community in which he moved. His book, published subsequent to the completion of his prison sentence, is entitled, 'I was wrong'. Its salutary challenge tells the story of a man who started in the centre of God's will and, from a position of favour, emigrated to the far country of personal ambition. One commentator summed up the six hundred pages of the book in a sentence when he said, 'Jim started out loving people and using things and ended up using people and loving things'. Jim Bakker learned his lesson the hard way but proves the point that a false focus can lead, all too quickly, to a fast fall. Favour with God can be found and favour with God can be lost, insofar as his anointing on us goes.

The day of favour

In one sense the world has been living in the day of God's favour for the past two millennia. At the commencement of his ministry Jesus went to the temple and, reading from the scroll of Isaiah, proclaimed, 'The Spirit of the Sovereign Lord is upon me, because he has anointed me to preach good news to the poor. He has sent me to proclaim freedom for the prisoners and recovery of sight for the blind, to release the oppressed, to proclaim the year of the Lord's favour.' We call this the day of grace – the period when God calls all men to be saved. It is the day of the open door to God's mercy. The past one hundred years have seen a heightened awareness of that favour as the prophecy of Joel 2 is being fulfilled and God is pouring out his Spirit on all flesh.

The return of Jesus is immanent, as God patiently waits to extend his mercy to all that will believe. The Bible says that in the last days two spiritual activities will operate globally. It speaks of a 'departing from the faith' as cults and heresy flourish but also of a time in which God will generously bestow unprecedented blessing across the earth – the most lavish expression of his favour thus far – a period culminating in his return.

Yet few things of value come without cost and God's favour is no exception for, while it can neither be earned nor deserved, there is a price for its retention.

This current move of God is something that calls for a fresh understanding of what holiness really means. Holiness is not the posturing of the religious Pharisee, drab and Bible black. It is attractive, magnetic and the only foundation to which the favour of God can be successfully secured. To quote the Psalmist,

> The Lord God is a sun and shield; the Lord bestows favour and honour; no good thing does he withhold from them whose walk is blameless (Ps. 84:11).

Yet, above almost everything else, God's favour is reserved for those who are willing to become vulnerable. People who are prepared to be broken and, like ploughed ground, thirsty for heaven's rain. The price of favour, if we were to consult Ezekiel, is a willingness to be 'ploughed and sown'. Most are willing for the seed of God's supply but few for the cutting instrument that breaks into hard earth to gain access for the seed.

Realizing that God *wants* to bless you, and *delights* to work through you, is the first step out of the snare.

However unfavourable the circumstances, refuse to accept the Devil's lie that you are limited by what you see. A circumstance is nothing more than the circle in which you are standing. You have been given the ability in God to break out of that circular perimeter fence.

I was once told that it was impossible for a Pentecostal service to be shown on prime-time television in Scotland. When I contacted the head of religious broadcasting it was confirmed that such a thing had never happened in the history of television broadcasting north of the border.

A couple of years later I felt that the 'acceptance' of this was a snare in which I seemed content to stay. It must be broken. Through a remarkable series of events a television crew agreed to survey our building on the understanding that there was no commitment to proceed.

When the day came my secretary came into my office to say that the people from the television company had arrived and, in the seconds before I met the potential producer, I reminded myself again that God's favour was part of my inheritance. As I shook the hand of the man who was the 'decision maker' the Lord gave me a 'word of knowledge' about an area of the man's life that it was impossible for me to have known about. I instantly shared it with him. He said he was amazed and suggested with a smile that I was 'winding him up' and that someone from the television company had phoned me in advance with this information. God gave us great favour with the whole team from that moment on and we received, not one, but three prime-time Sunday morning broadcasts.

Reader, it does not matter how low you feel, how far you fell before you came to Christ, how unworthy you consider yourself to be: if you are born again, the favour of God is part of your inheritance. Claim it. It's yours.

I love the story of Rahab. If God could bless her he can bless anyone. She was a common prostitute but 'believed God' could save her even though the rest of the city of Jericho had been designated for destruction. Of all the people in God's Word who qualify for the 'breaking free from small ambitions' award, she has to be on the short list.

Rahab did a deal with the spies that guaranteed that everyone of her family would be saved if she could get them into the same place of safety as herself – her house in the wall. She had never read the Bible, never attended a church service and never attended a discipling course. All she had was the faith that said if God could save her then he could save all those she loved. No wonder she is mentioned in the select group of heroes in the book of Hebrews and became part of the family tree of none other than Jesus himself.

Joshua said to the two men who had spied out the land, 'Go into the prostitute's house and bring her out and all who belong to her, in accordance with your oath to her.' So the young men who had done the spying went in and brought out Rahab, her father and mother and brothers and all who belonged to her. They brought out her entire family and put them in a place outside the camp of Israel.[5]

Of course God will favour whomsoever he wishes. Obviously God is sovereign in all his acts. He also responds to those who have the 'audacity to believe' that, as a Father, he loves them enough to provide for them.

A teachable spirit

Emancipation from small ambition is experienced by those who have a desire to grow and know that there is more to learn.

When Saul of Tarsus was confronted by Jesus on the road to Damascus, he asked two questions. The first was, 'Who are you Lord?' and the second, 'What shall I do Lord?' Coming to a knowledge of who God is must be followed by a desire to discover what he would have us do about what we now know.

When Jeremiah was told to go to the potter's house, God showed him the raw material with which he was working: malleable clay.[6] The vessel had a defect but, because the clay was soft, that was not an insurmountable problem. It could be re-shaped into the form that the potter had designed for it. That is exactly how God wants his Church to be.

It is not always noted however that in the next chapter Jeremiah is asked to return for another pottery lesson. This time the object he was asked to observe was a vessel that, having been fired in a kiln, was hard; its defects now irreversibly part of its make-up. God ordered that this vessel should be smashed. Sometimes the only thing that God can do with hearts that will not soften is to break them.

God is looking for people that are listening. He does not want to chisel into our intransigence but rather to write softly upon a parchment that is pliable and yielding.

> You show that you are a letter from Christ, the result of our ministry, written not with ink but with the Spirit of the living God, not on tablets of stone but on tablets of human hearts.[7]

An internationally-known boxer of a bygone era, when in his prime, was asked by a flight attendant to fasten his seat belt. With a knowing wink to his travelling companion he responded by saying, 'Sweetheart, superman need no seatbelt.' She quietly replied, 'Sir, superman need no plane.'

The intransigent always set themselves up for a fall.

There is something about a pastor's first church that is special. That was certainly true in my case. I was assigned as a young man to a small town in South Wales called Llantrisant. I can remember that on my first Sunday, there were seventeen people in the congregation and the weekly offering was £22.

In the small group was a young man of fifteen who had decided to learn to play the guitar. Over the next few years he developed into a very proficient musician and began writing his own songs. Nothing too spectacular about the story so far and little to distinguish him from thousands of others from churches small and large across the United Kingdom. The difference was that whenever, a quarter of a century later, I think of a 'teachable spirit' I think of him. When he wrote lyrics he did not assume them to be masterpieces just because they came from his pen. He would ask if they were biblically accurate or culturally relevant. And when he did so he did not look for people to confirm his prejudices but, if it was necessary, amended the compositions accordingly. It is no surprise to me that Noel Richards has become one of the finest composers and worship leaders in the world today.

As with so many snares, unteachableness not only affects the individual but those who could have been blessed through them if their spirit had been more open. We might well ask how anyone could get themselves into such a trap. The fact is that at the root of all unteachableness is rebellion.

A primary requirement for a prophet is that they have an open ear. They cannot convey to others what they have not heard from God. They have to have an instructed tongue. Isaiah makes it very clear that the opposite of spiritual listening is not deafness but rebellion:

> The Sovereign Lord has given me an instructed tongue, to know the word that sustains the weary. He wakens me morning by morning, wakens my ear to listen like one being taught. The Sovereign Lord has opened my ears, and *I have not been rebellious*; I have not drawn back (italics mine).[8]

Rebellion is at the root of all sin. It was at the core of Lucifer's fall from heaven to earth and Adam's fall from intimacy to exclusion. In Hebrews 3 there are five symptoms of spiritual rebellion.

Hardness of heart

As we have seen this occurs when one is 'set' against God.

Disobedience

The Lord . . . said:

> 'Go up and take possession of the land I have given you' but you rebelled against the command of the Lord your God. You did not trust him or obey him. You have been rebellious against the Lord ever since I have known you.[9]

Corrupt focus

The Living Bible paraphrases this as, 'They were always looking somewhere else instead of up to me'.

Spiritual ignorance

Though many that fall into this category pride themselves on their knowledge of the Scripture, God says of them 'they have not known my ways'.

Testing

This refers to a pushing of God to the limits of his grace. There are those who may feel that, as God does not immediately bring them into check when their rebellion is exercised, that in some way they have received his endorsement upon their actions. Like the Pharisees we shall consider later, the rebellious spirit often promotes itself as a defender of truth and guardian of tradition.

The book of Genesis refers to the sin of the Amorites 'not having yet reached its full measure'. Jesus warns the Pharisees, 'Fill up then the sin of your forefathers!' To the Thessalonian Church, Paul writes of those who 'heap up their sins to the limit. The wrath of God has come upon them at last.'[10]

Eventually everyone will sit down to a banquet of consequences. For the rebellious, according to the passage in Hebrews, this includes stirring up the anger of God, embracing curse into their lives and closing the door on what God would love to do through them – if only their heart had been open.

The worst result for the local church for those who act in rebellion to God's purpose is that, if left unchallenged, they can defile an entire congregation. This snare is one of the strongest and most devastating, so it is important that we consider it closely and carefully.

I am not referring here to those who differ from the leadership on some point of church practice or who occasionally feel that they are unable completely to endorse every decision that is made by them. Such points of variance are natural and part of family life. Given that pastors and elders are but mortal it may be that, when listening to those who have genuine concerns, helpful adjustments can be made for the better.

What we are focussing on here is those who are perpetually set against the direction the leadership of the church is taking. These people come to church on Sunday with a bitter spirit and leave with their attitudes more deeply entrenched. Their hearts are cold and their demeanour is sour.

A tiny group of such people can have a negative effect upon a church out of all proportion to their numbers. The reason for this is that the Enemy knows what a potent narcotic their presence is. There is a 'spirit that they are of' and if the leadership does not challenge this attitude by intercession and personal intervention the disease will most certainly spread. The power behind them is often demonic and they are exercising a level of control which is Satanic in origin. Those who think that witchcraft only has to do with broomsticks, voodoo masks and shamanism should look closer to home.

> Rebellion is like the sin of divination (Authorised Version witchcraft), and arrogance like the evil of idolatry.[11]

The 'acts of the sinful nature' listed in Galatians 5 have much to do with interpersonal relationships – hatred, discord, dissensions, factions and, numbered among them, 'witchcraft'.

It could be argued that a correct exegesis of the text in 1 Samuel would convey only that rebellion was 'as bad as' witchcraft in God's sight. What all would agree on is that rebellion has a pervasive and contagious controlling effect and this is seen most sharply in the account of Korah's rebellion.[12]

What began with four people spread to 250 until, finally, judgement had to be meted out on 14,700 people. It is said of the initial group that they 'became insolent and rose up against Moses'. We need to note that, in the same way that rebellion is paralleled with witchcraft, arrogance is contrasted with idolatry, the controlling idol being an independence that refuses to accept any other authority than its own. It is significant that the opening gambit of this group is a spiritual authority issue, 'You have gone too far! The whole community is holy, everyone of them, and the Lord is with them. Why do you set yourselves above the Lord's assembly?'

They perceive themselves as speaking on behalf of the whole of Israel though God has given them no anointing to represent the people or to lead.

As is so often the case when rebellion occurs, the presented argument is couched in spiritual language; but when we look closer we discover a far more basic motive for Korah's revolt. Could the insurrection have its roots much closer to home? We discover that Korah may well have harboured a hidden agenda of his own.

Korah was the cousin of Moses and Aaron and was of equal rank with Aaron in the tribe. Aaron however was High Priest and Korah was not. The real reason for the rebellion was Korah's wounded ego. He had fallen into the snare of sedition but, because he had such a corrupting and controlling influence, almost fifteen thousand people died as a consequence.

When church splits occur they do so for the most 'spiritual' of reasons. Those who are wise will look closer for the cause. Paul gave a warning to watch for motive when he spoke his last moving message to the Ephesian elders:

> I know that after I leave, savage wolves will come in among you and will not spare the flock. Even from your own number men will arise and distort the truth *in order to draw away disciples after them*. So be on your guard![13]

Though mercifully it has never happened in a church that I have pastored, I have witnessed the aftermath of what rebellious people leave in their wake when a rebellious coup collapses. The people who have followed them soon see the foolishness of uniting around a negative and discover that, rather than having been led into the Promised Land, they have been seduced into a desert. But what do the deluded disciples do?

Their river usually splits into one of four tributaries. The most honest of them return to their source in a spirit of repentance. Others know that they should do the same but, unwilling to lose face, drift off to other churches fully aware that this is not God's primary purpose for them. Another group may try to reform unaware that, as they were formed in dissension, they are likely to divide and divide again. The weaker ones become disillusioned by the payoff that schism brings and fail to go on with God. So often this happens all because one person felt that he was not getting the 'profile' that he deserved.

We have seen how Lucifer's fall affected those angels that followed him.

> The angels who did not keep their positions of authority but abandoned their own home – these he has kept in darkness, bound with everlasting chains for judgement on the great Day.[14]

Adam's demise, as federal head of the human race, brought death on all men and, had it not been for the faithfulness of the second and last Adam, we would all be under similar condemnation today.

Numbers 16 tells of a terrible irony in the method God used to bring judgement upon those who gullibly stepped into Korah's snare:

> . . . the ground under them split apart and the earth opened its mouth and swallowed them, with their households and all Korah's men and all their possessions. They went down alive into the grave, with everything they owned; the earth closed over them, and they perished and were gone from the community.

A trap of their own making was to snap shut over them for ever.

Moses, seeing that it was his authority that was at issue, sensibly stepped aside from the matter and left the judgement to God. Given that Moses was operating under delegated authority, it should be noted that it was God's government that was also being challenged.

Over recent years there has been a spate of medical scares in which those who had been tested for an illness have subsequently heard that the integrity of the examination procedures was being brought into question. Hospital telephone switchboards became jammed. Anxious callers pleaded for information about steps that they should take to ensure that their future was secure. What steps should you take if you are beginning to recognize that perhaps you are being drawn into a web of intrigue spun by someone who may have motives other than your best interest at heart?

The Bible makes it clear that the story of Korah's rebellion was not included in the canon of Scripture so that we would be more accurately appraised of the historical events of the period. The Scripture says that it is presented to us as a 'warning sign'.[15]

If we thought that everyone who saw a red light stopped, the world would be a safer place. Yet those who witnessed God's judgement in Korah's day were in such denial that they blamed Moses for 'killing the Lord's people'.

It may be that you have a friend or loved one who is in danger of being sucked into the vortex of someone else's ego and this chapter is coming as a timely word of warning. If that is the case, then the three words to be embraced are repent, refuse and reject.

Those who are carriers of a spirit of rebellion should repent before God and arrange to speak with those in authority with whom they have a problem.

Refuse to participate even by listening to words of bitterness and dissension. You will know of the experience of walking into a room, where there is an atmosphere of gossip and guile, and how you leave feeling polluted in spirit even though you have not participated.

> The words of a gossip are like choice morsels; they go down to a man's inmost parts.

> A perverse man stirs up dissension, and a gossip separates close friends.

> Without wood a fire goes out; without gossip a quarrel dies down.[16]

Do not have fellowship with those who have a rebellious spirit. When God was about to bring judgement, in the account of Korah's rebellion, he told Moses to warn the people to, '*Move away* from the tents (homes) of these wicked men. Do not touch anything belonging to them, *or you will be swept away because of all their sins*' (italics mine). That just shows how infectious insurrection is.

A millennium and a half later God had still not compromised this principle. To the church in Rome Paul writes:

> Watch out for those that cause divisions . . . Keep away from them.[17]

The wonderful news is that this cycle of sedition can be stopped. It is not necessarily a terminal illness.

Though judgement came upon Korah, some of his descendants survived. They were men of a different

spirit and seven hundred years later David used
them as his worship team. They became the authors
of thirteen of the Psalms. If you would like to study
the clear contrast between their attitude and the
spirit of their infamous ancestor then read at leisure
Psalms 44–49, 84,85,87,88.

Resisting the fear of failure

Snapping the snare of small ambition requires that
we deal with the fear of failure in our life. This can be
linked to the fear of man and also to pride. We do not
want to be seen in less than a perfect light. Jeremiah
speaks of not 'running away from being the shepherd' of those that God had put under his charge.
There are of course other more altruistic reasons
connected to a fear of failure, such as being aware of
the responsibility of serving the Lord and not wanting to fail others by doing less than our best.

There are times when we have to just 'go for it'.
When we believe that God has spoken, we must act
and leave the results to him. Steer clear of this snare
and live by faith rather than sight. If you do, then there
is no limit to what God can accomplish through you.

Some years ago Colin Dye and I were ministering
in Nigeria. During the opening weeks we had been
speaking at a convention in Ibadan, a city in the south
of the country. In the closing stages of the itinerary we
attended a series of meetings in a city to the north –
near the Sahara. The opening night saw around five
thousand people present for this great evangelistic
event.

During the day the organisers drew us to one side to inform us that they had reason to believe that we were in danger from Islamic extremists who had threatened to kill anyone who made a commitment to Christ.[18] Many Christians in the outlying villages, though incredibly poor by Western standards, had made provision to accommodate and feed an extra person for as long as was necessary. When it was thought safe the new convert could then make his way back to live in the city. The commitment of Nigerian believers in areas where their faith is under threat is outstanding by any standards.

Colin Dye spoke on the first evening and concluded with an appeal I shall never forget. Having clearly presented the gospel he invited those who were sick to come forward for prayer. There is nothing remarkable about that in a Pentecostal context. However, he then said to the hundreds who had made their way to the front, 'If Jesus heals blind eyes, opens deaf ears and makes the lame to walk then he is not dead; he is alive and he is Lord and you must believe in him. But if he does not do these things then don't believe in him: he is not alive and he is not Lord'.

Scores of people were healed. The lame walked, the blind saw and the deaf had their hearing restored. Then Colin asked those who had come forward to return to the place in the crowd from where they had come. Doing so they showed their friends and families the results of their healing. Later, when the appeal for salvation was made, even though the threat of death had been put upon them, nine hundred people responded to the call for salvation.

The temptation for the preacher not to be obedient, given all the pressures I have enumerated, was colossal. Because he overcame the fear of failure, hundreds were released from their personal snares of sin and sickness.

Yet it is not in huge meetings that such obedience is first tested. It happens the first time that a new convert considers whether he or she will pray publicly, witness for Christ, or exercise spiritual gifts.

When I was in my early teens I have memories of my father who was a minister, taking the young people to the park on a Sunday afternoon for an open-air service. The format was straightforward and rarely changed. Once a semicircle had been formed, guitarists would strike up 'choruses' then volunteers would give their testimonies.

Every Sunday, on the half-mile walk from church to park, I wrestled with the hope that I might have the courage to step out of the edge of the circle and speak. Week after week, on the return journey, the fourteen-year-old boy would saunter back home hoping that perhaps 'next time' he would be brave enough. I can remember the moment that it happened. As the leader invited folk to speak I teetered on the edge of the group like a swimmer with his toes at the tip of a springboard contemplating his first dive. I came to the conclusion that if I waited until I felt courageous enough, it would never happen. I stepped into the ring. I cannot recall what I said. I am sure it was less than striking. What mattered to me was that at last I was 'there'. I had taken a faltering step out of a snare from which I hoped never to return.

6

The Snare of the Pharisee

You shut the kingdom of heaven in men's faces. You yourselves do not enter, nor will you let those enter who are trying to.[1]

I have left this towards the end of the book as I believe the snare of religion to be the most deadly of all the traps that face contemporary evangelicalism. The damage it does to those who are its victim, and to those that they affect, is incalculable. It is a sin more prevalent in the church than immorality and it is, in my view, the greatest single hindrance to revival.

The word Pharisee comes from the Aramaic *perashiym* meaning 'separated'. The Pharisees emerged during the period that scans the four hundred-year gap between the Old and New Testaments and stood strongly against the paganism of Antiochus Epiphanes. They succeeded the Assideans or Chasidim the 'godly men' and were known for their patriotism and faithfulness to the covenant.

However, by the time of Christ they had degenerated into a group that epitomised the very worst of cold religious orthodoxy. Jesus warned his disciples against the 'yeast of the Pharisees'.[2] By doing so he exposed the permeating and evil influence that, like yeast in dough, spread secretly, silently yet certainly throughout the communities in which they operated.

To understand the bondage into which their followers were brought we need carefully to examine each of the ten sharp teeth on the jaws of their snare.

Blind[3]

> You blind guides! You strain out a gnat but swallow a camel.

I do not think that there is any congregation of people anywhere in the world that has successfully inoculated itself totally against the toxic poison of Pharisaism. None of us is totally immune from it and each of us can be a carrier if we are not careful. I believe the virus to be present in virtually every church.

On one Sunday morning I had just concluded my message from a passage in Nehemiah and we were about to go into a time of open worship during which we would take communion. I had spoken of Nehemiah examining the walls of Jerusalem with the implication that we might examine the walls of our lives for breaches in our spiritual security.

My associate pastor was presiding over the meeting as, one after another, people began to offer prayers that displayed a deep sense of honesty. The vulnerability of the first gave courage to the next to be real and so it went on. An invitation was given to those who felt it appropriate to make their way to the front and several did: spontaneously kneeling on the carpeted steps that led up to the platform area. Many of them were quietly weeping. It was a holy moment. Before long the entire front of the church was full.

The meeting was running late and, though we had distributed the bread and wine, we did not on that Sunday read the Scriptures during communion.

In the post during the following week I received an irate and anonymous letter that berated me for not having a Bible reading during the time of communion. Did I not see the need to read 1 Corinthians 11? How else, I was asked, would people see the need to examine themselves as they ate the bread or drank of the cup?

I do not think that I have read anything with more incredulity than I read that letter that day. Someone had scrupulously noticed the absence of a ritual while remaining totally blind to a crowd of people kneeling and weeping at the front subsequent to an audit of their spiritual lives.

Calvary itself gives the perfect example of sightless Pharisaism:

> Because the Jews did not want the bodies left on the crosses during the Sabbath, they asked Pilate to have the legs broken and the bodies taken down.[4]

They could see the infringement of a rule but were blind to the fact that they had just crucified the

Creator of the universe. Blind does not get much more blind than that.

Hypocritical[5]

Six times in one chapter Jesus calls them hypocrites – those who wear a mask and act a part. They were preoccupied with externals but ignorant of those things with which Jesus was concerned: the matters of the heart.

> Woe to you, teachers of the law and Pharisees, you hypocrites! You give a tenth of your spices – mint, dill and cummin. But you have neglected the more important matters of the law – justice, mercy and faithfulness. You should have practised the latter, without neglecting the former.

Jesus referred to them as whitewashed tombs – outwardly respectable, but inside full of dead men's bones. These words seem harsh until we realize that Christ could see the cancerous effect historical and contemporary Pharisees would have on the Body of Christ.

Status orientated[6]

Position was their passion. The holding of the office was more important than the ministry itself. They needed leadership more than leadership needed them because it was a platform from which to project their ego.

> Woe to you Pharisees, because you love the most important seats in the synagogues and greetings in the marketplaces.

> They love the place of honour at banquets and the most important seats in the synagogues; they love to be greeted in the marketplaces and to have men call them 'Rabbi'.

I have the abiding memory as a small boy of attending a meeting at which a powerful sermon was preached before the service had even started. The church was crowded and music was being played as the platform party made its way on to the stage. The guest speaker and the convenor approached the central section of the front row, as would be normal, and the rest filled up the remainder of the seats. Two young leaders caught my eye and it was evident even to me as a child that, there being only one seat left at the front, one of them would have to make their way to the next row – hardly ignominy and shame one would have thought. However, it must have appeared like relegation from the first division to them as they momentarily jostled for the one remaining place. I could see that I was not the only one to notice the split-second squabble, for a senior minister, who was already seated in the centre, got up and insisted that one of these young men take the place he had occupied. I could not recall the text that was later preached, but two young men and one small boy learned a lesson that night that they would never forget. For me, whenever I saw that older pastor again, wherever he sat became the top table as far as I was concerned. In God's economy the way up is the way down.

United States President Woodrow Wilson related how one of his maids approached him the day after the Secretary of State for Labour had resigned from the United States Cabinet. 'Mr Wilson', she said, 'I would like you to consider appointing my husband as the new Secretary of State for Labour.' Taken aback, Mr. Wilson replied, 'You must remember my dear that the Secretary of State for Labour is an important position that requires a big man.' The maid replied without a blush, 'But sir, if you made my husband the Secretary of State for Labour he would be a big man.'

Too often the church appoints leaders and then asks God to bless them rather than watching who God is blessing and subsequently making an appointment.

Legalistic[7]

Now the day on which Jesus had made the mud and opened the man's eyes was a Sabbath. Therefore the Pharisees also asked him how he had received his sight. 'He put mud on my eyes', the man replied, 'and I washed, and now I see.' Some of the Pharisees said, *'This man is not from God, for he does not keep the Sabbath.'*

It did not matter to them that a man had been miraculously healed; once again their concern was only for the infringement of a rule.

> The teachers of the law and the Pharisees brought in a woman caught in adultery. They made her stand before the group and said to Jesus, 'Teacher, this woman was caught in the act of adultery. In the Law Moses commanded us to stone such women. Now what do you say?' They were using this question as a trap, in order to have a basis for accusing him. But Jesus bent down and started to write on the ground with his finger. When they kept on questioning him, he straightened up and said to them, 'If any one of you is without sin, let him be the first to throw a stone at her.'

The reason why those with a religious spirit hated Jesus so much was that he saw through their duplicity. He was not so much concerned about their knowledge of the Scriptures as with the state of their lives. The above passages highlight their incredible arrogance in that, not only did they feel that they had 'caught' this woman but they now sought to 'trap' Jesus as well.

What Jesus wrote on the ground we are not told. I believe it could have been a number of things. Who would have cast the first stone if Jesus had written out the name of a woman with whom one of the accusers had had an illicit relationship? What if he had scribbled in the sand the name of a notorious inn at which one of them had recently booked a room. We need to note that Jesus did not say, 'Let him who is without the sin of adultery cast the first stone' but, 'without sin'. Any sin could have been written there. There are three occasions when we find God 'writing'. The first is the writing of the Law with a finger of fire. The second is with a shadowy finger on the wall at Belshazzar's feast. The other occasion is here. In each case men were called to account and terror was evoked. It is significant that, whatever the content was, those men trailed away, the oldest first, as trembling fingers allowed accusatory stones to fall silently from their hands.

Slayers of blessing[8]

There is something particularly vicious about the religious spirit. John the Baptist called the Pharisees a brood of vipers and their bite was every bit as lethal as the name suggests. Jesus went even further:

> You snakes! You brood of vipers! How will you escape being condemned to hell? Therefore I am sending you prophets and wise men and teachers. Some of them you will kill and crucify; others you will flog in your synagogues and pursue from town to town.

Pharisees defile the church and persecute and revile the prophetic voice. Religious people crucified Jesus and have sought to bludgeon blessing wherever it has occurred throughout history. Jesus represented revival to the Jews. Before he came they longed for him, but when he appeared, they sought to put him to death.

I have heard people who have never won a soul for Christ in their life ridicule the huge revival at Pensacola and wherever else the Lord is pouring out his Spirit. That thousands are being saved does not seem to matter to them at all. It does not fall within the parameters of their narrow expectations and therefore must be instantly dismissed.

Kilsyth, as mentioned in an earlier chapter, has seen more revivals than perhaps any other place on the planet. This tiny town of ten thousand people has experienced three major revivals in the past two hundred and fifty years. I have included in the appendix some of the details surrounding these remarkable demonstrations of the favour of God.

In the revival of 1732 in which many were saved, the historians record:

> Because there were many outward manifestations, strong wailing and falling down being two examples, Robe (a Church of Scotland minister) was charged with 'emotionalism'. Despite the fact that hundreds were saved, the religious establishment, as so often is the case, were unmoved by the power of God and spoke of the Revival as a 'Delusion and work of the Grand Deceiver'. Robe answered his critics by pointing out that Satan's works never yet produced reformation of life and manners and the embracing of the righteousness of God.

Each of the revivals had a similar assault from religious people who, like David's wife who criticized him when he danced before the Lord, were bequeathed barrenness for their sins.

I have encountered many modern-day Pharisees in my time, but in over thirty years of ministry, I have yet to meet one who is a soul-winner.

Those who embrace the spirit of the Pharisee also teeter on the edge of the precipice of the ultimate transgression: the unpardonable sin.

I have heard people dispute between themselves as to what constitutes that offence as if there were some doubt. The Bible makes in perfectly plain. It is the attributing to Satan of a work of grace that has been initiated by the Holy Spirit. Those religious souls who speak of 'tongues', spiritual gifts and other contemporary manifestations of God as originating from the Devil, sail very close to the wind. It is because this passage is so vitally important that I include it here in full:

Then they brought him a demon-possessed man who was blind and mute, and Jesus healed him, so that he could both talk and see. All the people were astonished and said, 'Could this be the Son of David?' But when the Pharisees heard this, they said, 'It is only by Beelzebub, the prince of demons, that this fellow drives out demons.' Jesus knew their thoughts and said to them, 'Every kingdom divided against itself will be ruined, and every city or household divided against itself will not stand. If Satan drives out Satan, he is divided against himself. How then can his kingdom stand? And if I drive out demons by Beelzebub, by whom do your people drive them out? So then, they will be your judges. But if I drive out demons by the Spirit of God, then the kingdom of God has come upon you. Or again, how can anyone enter a strong man's house and carry off his possessions unless he first ties up the strong man? Then he can rob his house. He who is not with me is against me, and he who does not gather with me scatters. And so I tell you, every sin and blasphemy will be forgiven men, but the blasphemy against the Spirit will not be forgiven. Anyone who speaks a word against the Son of Man will be forgiven, but anyone who speaks against the Holy Spirit will not be forgiven, either in this age or in the age to come.'[9]

The religious spirit also despises worship in which there is any semblance of life and vitality. As Jesus enters Jerusalem the people roar in adoration. The Pharisees were furious at such a show of emotion and devotion and called on Jesus to rebuke his disciples. Instead Jesus chastises them with the revelation that the stones would get a voice of their own if people were not allowed to praise. The inference was that those granite spheres possessed more tenderness than the callous hearts that criticized the worshippers.

Frances Frangipane in his book, *In the Presence of God* writes:

'When the Magi asked Herod about the star, they were amongst those who said that the Messiah would be born in Bethlehem. The Magi travelled eight hundred miles and discovered the Messiah. The Pharisees did not even bother going six miles down the road. They could have walked there in less than three hours. The difference was that though the Pharisee had doctrine and Law the Magi had come to worship'.[10]

Self-righteous[11]

The symbol of the Pharisee is a sneer. It is character-
ised by a super-spirituality that looks down on
anyone and everyone who does not meet their
particular benchmark of truth. The religious spirit is
arrogant in the extreme. Not only does it call true
believers to account but, when manifested while
Jesus was on Earth, had the temerity to call Christ to
account also.

> The Pharisees and the teachers of the law were looking
> for a reason to accuse Jesus, so they watched him closely
> to see if he would heal on the Sabbath.

Jesus never 'hit the wall' when he confronted the religious spirit. He addresses the parable of the Pharisee
and the tax collector to 'some who were confident of
their own righteousness and looked down on everybody else':

> 'Two men went up to the temple to pray, one a Pharisee
> and the other a tax collector. The *Pharisee stood up and
> prayed about himself*: . . .'

The final phrase in the quote says it all. If anyone falls
into the snare of the unteachable spirit then the
Pharisee does. There is nothing that you can teach
him – nothing more she needs to learn.

Their superior spirit 'demanded signs' and
selected Jesus' social circle for him by scrutinising
his dinner guests. They had the impudence to
cross-question the Word on points of doctrine, while

becoming quickly offended on any occasion that they were challenged.

I have always considered that one of the greatest miracles in the gospel narrative is that Jesus always contained himself when challenged by such confrontations. Had such things happened to us, the worst thing we could have done would have been to explode in self-defence. How much more a victor over temptation was Jesus who could have destroyed them with a single breath?

Locked into yesterday[12]

> Woe to you, teachers of the law and Pharisees, you hypocrites! You build tombs for the prophets and decorate the graves of the righteous. And you say, '*If we had lived in the days of our forefathers . . .*' (italics mine).

There is a verse in Ecclesiastes that Pharisees of all eras should consider, for those who have a religious spirit are inevitably shackled to the past:

> Do not say, 'Why were the old days better than these?' For it is not wise to ask such questions.

Why is it not wise? Perhaps because, not only do most of us have remarkably selective memories, but we also have the capacity, if we are not careful, of rewriting history in a hue that is far brighter than reality would allow. In short, people sometimes 'remember' things that never happened and history acquires a rosier glow with the passing of time. As the Lennon and McCartney lyric says, 'Yesterday, all our problems seemed so far away'.

Contemporary Pharisees find themselves in a dilemma when they witness on one hand the change that they resist and despise, and on the other, the life, vitality, growth and blessing all around them. Yet even this neither convinces nor deters them in their intransigent stance. On one occasion I met a bemused new convert who had just been told, 'It's all right you saying you have become a Christian but you should have got saved in my day; things were better then.'

It is certainly important that we should respect our roots, yet we should be influenced by our past rather than determined by it.

The problem is that 'change' is threatening. Psychologists tell us that most people perceive change as loss. Some feel that change will push their church into something that does not fit who they are. When *we* create change we are all for it. When others create change we are resistant. We see *them* as having 'more power' than *us* and *they* are creating a change that *we* have to live by. Bernard Shaw is quoted as saying, 'The reasonable man endeavours to adjust himself to the world. The unreasonable man seeks to adjust the world to himself. Therefore the future belongs to the unreasonable man'.

When we discover people who are sacrificially committed to breaking free from the snare of the status quo and will seek to adjust the world to God through the reconciling work of Jesus, revival will not be far away.

Perhaps the saddest thing is that yesterday's entrepreneurs and pioneers can turn all too quickly from fiery radicals to anxious reactionaries.

When Ford created the mass-produced motor car, and joked that it could be driven in any colour as long as it was black, he was present at the birth of a revolutionary concept. When, however, in later years, his production manager suggested that the sun was setting on the model T, he promptly sacked him. That done, he made his way to the garage and smashed up the gleaming red machine, ripping off its doors.

God help us not to become spiritual Luddites.

The phrase, 'If it isn't broke don't fix it' sounds common sense until we begin to examine the statement. If that thesis were true you would be reading this book by the light of sophisticated candles and worshipping on Sunday to the sound of a 'state of the art' harmonium.

Unless we change what we've got we will always remain what we are. To doubters, change is threatening because they worry that things will get worse. To the man or woman of faith, change is encouraging because they feel that things will get better.

To quote Frangipane, 'Too many people go through life umbilically tied to the protection of the familiar. Many stay in lifeless churches because of the security of familiar faces rather than the truth of Christ. Some choose dead religion so that they will not have to change.'

Some believe that reaction to change is a modern phenomenon. The phrase, 'The only permanent thing in life is change' was not uttered by a modern business guru but by Heraclitus in 700 BC.

When D.L. Moody went to Sunderland in 1874 pamphlets were posted on public buildings headed, 'Kindly thoughts on this religious movement'. These pamphlets proceeded to describe the singing of solos as 'the parading of human conceit' and Sankey's accordion as, 'a devilish pump machine that wheezes out blasphemies'. One wonders what 'kindly thoughts' would be addressed to the high-tech digital sophistication of our modern praise bands!

The Pharisee tended to put the Talmud (the Pharisee's theological commentaries) on a par with the Torah (the first five books of the Bible). Jesus was not so confused – hence their opposition to his teaching. He made a point of violating the traditions of the elders on a regular basis. Only doctrines are eternal. Traditions tarnish with the passing of time. Traditions are helpful only in so far as they serve us. A tenet generally accepted by equestrians is that if the horse is dead – dismount.

Charles Handy in his book, *The Empty Raincoat* observes, 'If you ask an Englishman why he does something, he replies "because". If you ask the same question to an American he is likely to say, "In order to".'[13] One statement looks back and the other forward. If a tradition assists us in the accomplishing of godly goals then that tradition should be retained. If it does not, then it has passed its sell-by date and should be discarded.

When the people of God sinned they were tormented by a plague of snakes. To highlight their repentance Moses made a serpent of brass and put it on a pole. Bronze is often a symbol of judgement in

Scripture, and the command to 'look and live' in order to be saved revealed the necessity of acknowledging the consequences of sin together with its cause. Jesus was to draw this parallel when prophesying of the impending cross:

> Just as Moses lifted up the snake in the desert, so the Son of Man must be lifted up, that everyone who believes in him may have eternal life.[14]

Yet centuries later people were still harking back to the 'old days' when miracles 'really happened'. They had started to give homage to a snake rather than the Saviour. It is significant that outbreaks of retrospection occur in direct proportion to the absence of anything worthy of note today.

And then it happened: Hezekiah . . . broke into pieces the bronze snake Moses had made, for up to that time the Israelites had been burning incense to it.

Given that in some churches a nuclear alert is sounded if a piece of church furniture is moved two metres to one side, one can only surmise the irate letters, anonymous and otherwise, that Hezekiah would have received in respect of this heinous act of sacrilege. The Scripture then says that he added more fuel to the fire by calling it 'Nehushtan' – just a piece of brass.

Like a later reformer Hezekiah recoiled from the tendency to venerate valuables – whether they were idolatrous ecclesiastical icons or the materialism at the extremes of prosperity teaching. It is the Christ of the cross, not the cross of Christ that is to be worshipped and adored. In the New Testament we

find no sacred sites and holy things – only sacred
Scripture and a holy people.

Thank God for the intervention of courageous
leadership that 'grasps the nettle' of neglected duty.
Because of Hezekiah, the seven hundred-year-old
snare was snapped.

Abandoned destiny[15]

When people live in their past they abandon their
future. Time and time again Jesus longed to emanci-
pate the Pharisees from the aridity of their lives.
With tears coursing down his cheeks he cries:

> O Jerusalem, Jerusalem, you who kill the prophets and
> stone those sent to you, how often I have longed to
> gather your children together, as a hen gathers her
> chicks under her wings, but you were not willing. Look,
> your house is left to you desolate.

Throughout the Bible the stark contrast between
relationship and barrenness is highlighted:

> God sets the lonely in families, he leads forth the prison-
> ers with singing; but the rebellious live in a
> sun-scorched land.

> Why should you be beaten anymore? Why do you per-
> sist in rebellion? Your whole head is injured, your
> whole heart afflicted. From the sole of your foot to the
> top of your head there is no soundness – only wounds
> and welts and open sores, not cleansed or bandaged or
> soothed with oil.

The most powerful and chilling passage is sent with laser-like accuracy by Luke the physician as he gives his prognosis on the disease of Pharisaism:

> The Pharisees and experts in the law rejected God's purpose for themselves.

Zealous[16]

The modern Pharisee's influence on a church is never neutral or passive. It is a spirit that always endeavours to proselytize. Of them Jesus said:

> Woe to you, teachers of the law and Pharisees, you hypocrites! You travel over land and sea to win a single convert, and when he becomes one, you make him twice as much a son of hell as you are.

They will go for anyone who will give them an ear. Everyone is a target whether they be a seasoned church member or first-time visitor to a church. The Pharisee cannot stand neutrality in others. Their world is divided starkly into allies and enemies. This brings us to the last of the ten teeth in this trap, and one that integrates itself with every other sharp incisor.

Controlling[17]

One of the most important things to the Pharisee is their power-base. Those that they can not bring

under their control they will endeavour to destroy.
Saul of Tarsus is a prime example and one who
described himself as, 'a Hebrew of Hebrews; in
regard to the law a Pharisee, as for zeal, persecuting
the church.'

Only minutes before his conversion we read this
of him:

> Meanwhile, Saul was still breathing out murderous
> threats against the Lord's disciples. He went to the high
> priest and asked him for letters to the synagogues in
> Damascus, so that if he found any there who belonged
> to the Way, whether men or women, he might take
> them as prisoners to Jerusalem . . . persecuted the
> followers of this Way *to their death*, arresting both men
> and women and throwing them into prison, as also the
> high priest and all the Council can testify. I even
> obtained letters from them to their brothers in Damas-
> cus, and went there to bring these people as prisoners to
> Jerusalem to be punished (italics mine).

Church leadership cannot ignore this religious
spirit in the hope that it will go away of its own
accord. It must first be addressed in the spiritual
realm from which its power emanates. It should
be confronted through teaching and, if that does
not have the required effect, through church discipline.

A note of caution: we must be wary of classifying
everyone who does not go along with our own
point of view as a Pharisee. Such an attitude can
become an immobilising snare in itself.

Hope for the Pharisee

Yes, there is hope. Even Pharisees are not beyond redemption. The Apostle Paul serves as the greatest example of someone who had his snare shattered – though it took a bolt from heaven to do it. Knocked off his high horse he lands at the feet of Jesus and rises to become one of the greatest Christian leaders that the world has ever seen. He contrasts with his namesake, the Saul of the Old Testament who started off at the centre of the will of God and slid to the margins, while Saul the Pharisee commences at the circumference and eventually arrives at the centre of God's plan for his life.

Many of us struggle with multiple snares in the course of a lifetime and Nicodemus wrestled with at least three. In one of the most famous passages in the New Testament we find him coming to see Jesus at night. The fact that he came at all was evidence that he had escaped, to some degree, the trap of unteachability. The Pharisee always finds it hard to come to the conclusion that he or she knows less than everything about everything.

That he came at night would indicate that he still was locked into the fear of what other people might think.

Even an evening encounter with Jesus did not set him fully free. When the Lord is hauled before the Sanhedrin (the Jewish ruling council of which Nicodemus was a member) Nicodemus finds himself able to proffer only a few weak words of support:

'Does our law condemn anyone without first hearing
him to find out what he is doing?'[18]

As with every snare, it was at the cross where freedom was finally realized. But first we need to look at
another powerful social figure. When Mark's Gospel
designates him as a 'member of the council', some
commentators conclude that he too was a member of
the Sanhedrin. Others deduce from this phrase that
his power was political and that the 'council'
referred to was a secular body chaired by Pilate.
What we do know about him however is that he was
locked into at least two snares. We know he was rich
and that, though a disciple, he was reticent to make
his faith public for 'fear of the Jews'. We may not be
wrong therefore in assuming that materialism and
the fear of man were the two traps into which he was
set.

Calvary was to make the difference. The two men
were part of the same crowd that surged and seethed
around the three impaled figures, although it was
the cross at the centre upon which most eyes were
concentrated.

The hands that had touched the rotting flesh of
the lepers and healed them were now nailed down.
The feet that had gone into the homes of rich and
poor alike were hammered firmly into place. The
face that had beamed upon the fallen countenance
of the harlot and given her hope was etched in
streams of blood. The Messiah was laid bare for the
world to see; fastened to two intersected pieces of
timber. Pilloried like a criminal and, in the greatest

irony in the universe, impaled like an animal caught in a snare.

The eyes of Nicodemus dart from the pulped face of the Messiah whose 'visage had been marred more than any man', to the jeering religionists who challenged Jesus to come down and save himself. Joseph's eyes scanned the crowd and recognized those among them whose opinions had already nailed his witness to the wall.

Nicodemus thought of the secret encounter that he was 'prepared to have' with Jesus at night and compared it to the willingness of that same Jesus to be crucified naked before a gaping world. Joseph became ashamed of what he had thought he would lose by identification with Jesus and contrasted it with all that Jesus had given for him.

Both of them looked at the cross and then, averting their gaze, their eyes locked into one another. They now knew what had to be done. Whether they had come together to Calvary that day we know not. What we do know is that they went away resolute and 'as one'. They had come to the realization that sin had nailed him down so that Pharisees like them could go free.

> Later, Joseph of Arimathea asked Pilate for the body of Jesus. Now Joseph was a disciple of Jesus, but secretly because he feared the Jews. With Pilate's permission, he came and took the body away. He was accompanied by Nicodemus, the man who earlier had visited Jesus at night. Nicodemus brought a mixture of myrrh and aloes, about seventy-five pounds.[19]

Both these men were leaders. The literal meaning of
'Nicodemus' is 'conqueror of men'. Before any
leader can effectively exercise authority over others,
he should seek to attain victory over the snares that
prevail in his own experience. His, or her, feet must
be the first to be unencumbered.

7

Free to Fly

There is a hunger around the world for revival – real, lasting, deep-rooted spiritual change. We have witnessed the superficial and the transient and nothing less than God's best will do. We have become, to use Tommy Tenney's phrase, 'God-chasers'.

This book commenced with the premise that, while we wait for God to act and 'set loose' his power, he is hitting the ball back into the court of the Church.

We call, like the psalmist, for God to 'roll his sleeves up':

Why do you hold back your hand, your right hand? Take it from the folds of your garment . . .[1]

But it is God who is calling the church into action. In Isaiah's day the cry was:

Awake, awake! Clothe yourself with strength, O arm of the LORD; awake, as in days gone by, as in generations of old.[2]

There is a sense in which you could not blame Israel for calling desperately on God in the same way that, from a human perspective, we can understand the disciples in a waterlogged boat frantically prevailing upon the Lord to come to their aid. From their vantage point, Jesus was laying on a soft cushion while their world was going under. Jesus did rise up and he did rebuke the waves, but the story does not end without him reprimanding them for *their* lack of faith.

The reply to the call upon God in Isaiah is immediately answered by him:

> For I am the Lord your God, who churns up the sea so that its waves roar – the Lord Almighty is his name. I have put my words in your mouth and covered you with the shadow of my hand – I who set the heavens in place, who laid the foundations of the earth, and who say to Zion, You are my people.[3]

And then adds, 'Awake, awake! Rise up, O Jerusalem'.

It is the church that is asleep and ensnared, not God. The cry is not, 'If God was interested, why does he not do something . . .' but, 'If my people who are called by my name will humble themselves . . .'

The key comes in the opening verses of the chapter that follows:

> Awake, awake, O Zion, *clothe yourself* with strength. Put on your garments of splendour, O Jerusalem, the holy city . . . Shake off your dust; rise up, sit enthroned, O Jerusalem. *Free yourself from the chains on your neck, O captive Daughter of Zion* (italics mine).[4]

Zion was immobile because, to a large extent, Zion was ensnared.

Clothe yourself

The Christian's wardrobe is packed with garments, all of which carry the designer label of heaven.

Though Peter directed a passage primarily to women,[5] the truth applies equally to men in that the *haute couture* of the heart impresses God far more than the outward adornment of Armani, Gucci or Versace.

To the Romans Paul writes about the importance of being 'clothed with Christ' and to the Galatians adds that this has to do with being baptised into him.

Consider four people who are about to be baptised by total immersion. The first two are men. One is a highly educated Oxford don and the second a man with only a basic education. The first woman is a wealthy socialite and the other, one of the poorest people in the community. Prior to their baptism they are easily distinguishable: the men by their vocabulary and turn of phrase, the women by their clothes and hairstyle.

Subsequent to baptism one is aware only of the element into which they have been immersed. In short, they are wet. All other distinguishing traits, including the expensive hairstyle, are reduced to one common denominator. Baptism is a great leveller. It is meant to be. It is a symbol of death to the flesh and the birth of the spirit.

So it is with those who have been baptised into Christ. Instead of the unearned acceptance of fashion and style it is Jesus, the element into which we have been immersed, that is revealed.

Paul describes this transformation to the Ephesians as 'putting on a new self'. And to the Colossians he itemises each individual garment by giving it its own name while collectively calling them the 'garments of salvation'.

To the Romans and Ephesians he highlights the clothes of the warrior. Jesus spoke, prior to Pentecost, about the importance of being clothed with power as Isaiah had referred to the apparel of praise – clothes for every eventuality.[6]

The popularity of terms such as 'power dressing' and 'dress for success' reveal the culture that articulates that people wear clothes to make a statement. That is no less true in the world of the Spirit. Whether or not we are clothed with Christ affects how the world sees us, how the Father sees us, and how the Devil sees us.

Imagine that I am walking down the street and you come up behind me and touch me on the shoulder. In reality you are not actually touching 'me' at all – you are touching what clothes me – my jacket or coat. When the Devil tries to 'get to you' he's got to go through God first. Ask Job.

The basis of our security is that our lives are 'hidden in Christ in God'.

This also means that we have to be careful how we treat one another. God said of his Old Testament people that those that 'touched' them touched the 'apple of his eye'.[7] In other words, coming against them was like prodding a stick in God's face and affecting the most sensitive part of the body – the pupil.

There is no evidence that Saul of Tarsus ever met Jesus, but when he was arrested on the Damascus road on his way to imprison and torture believers, the charge brought against him was, 'Saul, Saul why do you persecute *me*'.[8]

Shake off the dust

We all at some time in our lives have overslept. I have never heard of anyone who has slept so long that they have gathered dust. God says that that was how long his people had been rendered immobile and in slumber. And let us not forget; these were the very ones who were telling *him* to wake up!

Rise Up. It's time for action. It's time to take up your bed and walk.

Sit enthroned. Come to terms with who you are in Christ. You are not a slave to be chained to a wall but a son abounding in authority.

> The Lord your God, who is going before you, will fight for you, as he did for you in Egypt, before your very eyes, and in the desert. There you saw how *the Lord your God carried you, as a father carries his son*, all the way you went until you reached this place (italics mine).[9]

A mother carries a child in her arms but a father carries his son on his shoulders. We are seated with him in heavenly places.

All of these imperative commands are our responsibility to implement. God does not say, 'Sit still while I dress you', he says instead, 'Put on the whole armour of God'. God never does anything for us that we can do for ourselves.

When Jesus was informed that Lazarus was dead he made his way to the tomb. Before his friend could experience the liberty that was to be his destiny, the account in John 11 reveals three obstacles that had to be removed. The first was the stone that lay across the cave where the corpse had been placed. Jesus called for them to move the stone away. This was not because he was incapable of doing this miraculously – after all, an angel was going to roll away a stone from his own tomb only a few weeks later.

The second was the need to call Lazarus to 'come forth'. This was something that only he could do, so he did it.

The third was the need as Lazarus emerged from the darkness, to have his grave clothes removed. Removing the garments of death required not an instant miracle, but a dedicated devotion. It mirrored the painstaking commitment of millions yet to come who would involve themselves in the discipling of those who, one day, would be born again.

Now, because God and man co-operated in a miracle, Lazarus was released from the bondage that had held him fast. He was free to fly.

The call now is for the church, at the beginning of the twenty-first century, to be similarly loosed into the destiny that God has planned for them.

The Spirit of God calls to you . . . 'Come fly with me'.

The woman was given the two wings of a great eagle, so that she might fly to the place prepared for her . . . out of the serpent's reach (Rev. 12:14).

Notes

Chapter 1

1   Ps. 111:10.

2   Prov. 10:27; 16:6; 24:4; Acts 9:31.

3   A man had a dream of a group of climbers at the bottom of a steep cliff. As he watches, he notices that a number of the group begin to climb while the others remain motionless. Those remaining at the base of the cliff now divide into two sections. The first group call up to the climbers with words of encouragement. Though not climbing themselves they are thrilled at the progress of their friends and point out to them footholds and ledges that will advance their headway. The second group at the base of the cliff have come to the conclusion that every metre that the climbers are making is a metre that advertises their own lack of progress. The solution, as they see it, is to shoot the climbers down with bullets of discouragement. Picking them off one by one, and watching them fall to the valley floor they sneer, 'You thought you could move ahead of me but there is no distance between us now'.

4   Lk. 23:11,12.

5   It is said that a fox in a snare will become so desperate that it will bite off its own paw to be free. The pain of

staying put and dying is worse than the pain of losing a limb, and going free. Mt. 5:30: 'If your right hand causes you to sin, cut it off and throw it away. It is better for you to lose one part of your body than for your whole body to go into hell'.

6 Ps. 25:15.
7 Rom. 12:3; Jas. 2:9.
8 For further reading into the revivals of Kilsyth read, *Miners, Weavers and the Open Book* by James Huchieson, Kelvinprint, 1986.
9 Harry Tee was the author of the hymn, 'I want my life to be all filled with praise to Thee', *Redemption Hymnal* 610.
10 The church wanted to affiliate with both Elim and Assemblies of God as they had close fellowship with both. At that time however the constitution of Assemblies of God did not allow a church to be in mutual affiliation. They made the decision to choose a minister and then affiliate to the group with which he was in relationship.

Chapter 2

1 Studies in the USA reveal that by the time children reach the age of fourteen they will have witnessed 18,000 murders on television, and by the time they leave school they will have spent more time in front of a television set at home than in the classroom. 22% of American adults polled admit to the fact that they would find it hard to live without television. In the UK the average time that an adult admits to watching television is twelve hours per week – equivalent to around eight years of waking life in front of the box.
2 1 Tim. 6:6–10.
3 Hodder & Stoughton, 1978.

Chapter 3

1. Acts 14:11–18.
2. Acts 28:1–6.
3. Lk. 19:35–40.
4. Dan. 10:1–19.
5. Regal Books, 1994.
6. See P. Billheimes *Destined for The Throne*, Christian Literature Crusade, 1975.
7. Ps. 68:18; Jas. 5:16.
8. 1 Sam. 3 and 1 Sam. 2:29. The book *Open Heart, Open Hands* was published by Marshall Pickering, London, 1988, now out of print.
9. 1 Pet. 3:7.
10. Eph. 4:25–27.
11. Prov. 7:17–27.
12. 1 Cor. 10:12–13. Living Bible.
13. Mt. 6:14–15.
14. 1 Cor. 11:27–32.
15. Mt. 5:23–24; 1 Cor. 11:23.

Chapter 4

1. Jas. 3:3–6.
2. Prov. 27:6.
3. Prov. 10:11.
4. 1 Chr. 4:9–10.
5. Prov. 12:18.
6. Prov. 20:19 and see also 11:13; 16:28; 18:8; 26:20,22.
7. Prov. 16:32.
8. Mt. 12:36–37.
9. Acts 5:1.
10. Gen. 15:11.
11. Eccl. 5:2–6; Prov. 20:25.
12. Deut. 18:19–22.
13. Jer. 14:14.

Chapter 5

1   Jas. 3:1; Heb. 13:17.
2   Heb. 4:2; Num. 13.
3   Josh. 14:10–12.
4   Part of the section on the favour of God was first published by the author in an article in *Direction*, the magazine of the Elim Pentecostal churches in Great Britain. It is reproduced here with their permission. Some of the ancillary texts applicable to this section are: Acts 10:34; Rom. 2:10,11; Eph. 6:9; Col. 3:25; Mt. 17:1; Mk. 5:37; 14:33; Gal. 2:9; Gen. 4:4; 6:8; Neh. 5:19; Lk. 1:30; Gen. 39:4; 15:11; Ex. 32:11; 1 Sam. 2:26; 2 Chr. 7:14; 2 Cor. 6:2; Lk. 4:18,19; Ezek. 5:11; Ps. 84:11; Ezek. 36:8,9; Hos. 10:12.
5   Josh. 2:1; 6:22–23; Heb. 11:31; Mt. 1:5.
6   Jer. 18:1ff; 19:1ff.
7   2 Cor. 3:2–3.
8   Isa. 50:4–5.
9   Deut. 9:22–24.
10 Gen. 15:16; Mt. 23:32–33; 1 Thess. 2:16.
11 1 Sam. 15:23.
12 Num. 16.
13 Acts 20:29–31.
14 Jude 6.
15 Num. 26:10.
16 Prov. 18:8; 16:28; 26:20.
17 Rom. 16:17.
18 In an evangelistic outreach held in the region by Reinhard Bonnke some months later, religious extremists attacked the crowd and many lost their lives. The outreach that the story refers to was sponsored by 'Sword of the Spirit Ministries', the chairman of which is Dr Frances Waleoke.

Chapter 6

[1] Mt. 23:13.
[2] Mt. 16:6.
[3] Mt. 23:24.
[4] Jn. 19:31.
[5] Mt. 23.
[6] Lk. 11:43; Mt. 23:6–7.
[7] Jn. 9:16; Mt.12:2; Mk. 2:18; Jn. 8:3–7.
[8] Mt. 3:7; 12:14; 23:33,34; Mk. 3:6; Lk. 11:53.
[9] Mt. 12:22–32; 9:24; Lk. 19:39.
[10] New Wine Ministries (1994).
[11] Lk. 16:15; 18:9–11; 6:7; Mt. 12:38; 9:11; 19:3; 15:12; Mk. 2:16; 3:5.
[12] Mt. 23:29–30; Ecc. 7:10.
[13] Arrow Paperbacks, 1995.
[14] Num. 21; Jn. 3:14,15; 2 Kgs. 18:4.
[15] Mt. 24:37,38; Ps. 68:6; Isa. 1:5,6; Lk. 7:30.
[16] Mt. 23:15.
[17] Phil. 3:5,6; Acts 9:1,2; 22:4; 5,19.
[18] Jn. 7:51.
[19] Jn. 19:38–40.

Chapter 7

[1] Ps. 74:11.
[2] Isa. 51:9.
[3] Isa. 51:15–17.
[4] Isa. 52:1,2.
[5] 1 Pet. 3:4.
[6] Rom. 13:14; Gal. 3:27; Eph. 4:22; Col. 3:9–12; Rom. 13:12; Eph. 6:13; Lk. 24:49; Isa. 61:3; 1 Cor. 15:50–56.
[7] Zech. 2:8.
[8] Acts 9:24.
[9] Deut.1:30–31.

Appendix

Kilsyth – Heartland of Revival

There must be very few places on earth that have experienced as many significant moves of God as have occurred in Kilsyth, Scotland. In the past two hundred and fifty years this small town, with a population of under ten thousand has experienced no less than three major revivals.

The revival of 1742

The first revival occurred in 1742, a period in Scottish history that most would associate with Bonnie Prince Charlie. Just prior to the outbreak in Kilsyth, George Whitefield, writing in a letter dated 19 July records:

> At mid-day I came to Cambuslang, and preached at 2 p.m. to a vast body of people; again at 6 p.m. and again at nine at night. Such commotions surely were never heard of especially at eleven o'clock at night. For an hour and a half there was much weeping and so many falling into such deep distress, expressed in various

ways as cannot be described. The people seemed to be
slain in scores. Their agonies and cries were exceed-
ingly affecting. Mr McCulloch preached, after I had
done, till 1 a.m. in the morning; and they could not
persuade the people to depart. In the fields all night
might be heard the voices of prayer and praise.

He refers to the scene in his writings as likened to a
battlefield in which the wounded were supported by
their friends as they were unable to stand unaided.

This revival was shortly to impact Kilsyth but, for
the moment, we must step back ten years to encounter James Robe, the Kilsyth Parish minister, a man
who had preached to his congregation for over thirty
years without any apparent success. During these
years of apathy and lethargy Robe prayed earnestly
for a descent of the Holy Spirit and had set up a
seven-year concert of prayer for revival.

In 1732 Kilsyth was stricken by a pleuritic fever
which claimed sixty lives in just six weeks. A few
months later devastating flooding swept away
houses, drowned livestock and destroyed most of
the cornfields. Eyewitnesses testify to hailstones falling which were three inches in circumference.
Added to this, James Robe encountered opposition
within his church and a number of people left. When
famine ravaged the town and left people on the brink
of starvation, it seemed that revival could not have
been further away.

Robe however was tenacious and held on to God.
His prayers were answered. Revival fires descended
on the town. The impact of the revival on society as a
whole was soon felt. However, because there were

many outward manifestations, strong wailing and falling down being two examples, Robe was charged with 'emotionalism'. Despite the fact that hundreds were saved, the religious establishment, as so often is the case, were unmoved by the power of God and spoke of the revival as a 'delusion and work of the Grand Deceiver'.

Robe answered his critics by pointing out that Satan's works never yet produced reformation of life and manners and the embracing of the righteousness of God.

The revival of 1839

In the first quarter of the nineteenth century Kilsyth had hardened to the gospel to the point that it was said that, 'The Apostle Paul would not be able to get the people of Kilsyth out to a full meeting on three Sabbaths running'.

However, this was to change. William Chalmers Burns, a young man twenty-four years of age was led to preach on the subject of revival. He read from Acts 2 and then preached from Psalm 110:3, 'Thy people shall be willing in the day of Thy power'. As he ministered, people broke forth in uncontrollable wailing and tears and groans intermingled with shouts of joy and praise. Some screamed and others fell to the ground as if dead. The meeting eventually concluded at 3 a.m. having lasted five hours.

The revival had begun and, when he preached a few days later, he found himself preaching to a thousand people on a Saturday afternoon. The next day he preached for two hours to a crowd of ten thousand people. Another large service was planned that evening and yet another at 10 p.m. This meeting lasted till 3 a.m. Some who had been counselled did not leave until 6 a.m.

One man commenting on the impact of this move of God recorded, 'The web became nothing to the weaver, nor the forge to the blacksmith, nor his bench to the carpenter, nor his furrow to the plough-man. They forsook all to crowd the churches and the prayer meetings'. It was commonplace for hundreds to meet for early morning prayer in the market square before going to work.

Once again religious people opposed the move of God and, once again, the fruits bore eloquent and indisputable testimony to its genuineness.

Burns went as a missionary to China in 1846 and laboured there for over twenty years. He was a source of encouragement to the young Hudson Taylor who was later to found the China Inland Mission. A missionary on furlough was asked if he had ever known William Burns, 'Know him, sir,' he replied, 'Every man in China knows him! He is the holiest man alive.'

Once again God had chosen to pour out his Spirit on the small town of Kilsyth but there were still more remarkable visitations yet to come.

The revival of 1908

The Kilsyth Chronicle of 12 June 1897 announced meetings that would be taking place in the Westport

Hall which were specifically intended 'to meet the wants of the non-church goer'.

At the turn of the century, poverty was rife in the town and Kilsyth had some of the worst housing stock in Britain during that period. Established churches in the town were having great difficulty in integrating the largely mining community into church life. To their credit, local ministers supported the formation of a new fellowship and in 1902 a committee of four elders and four deacons was appointed. The designated name of the church was 'Church of God, Kilsyth'.

When revival fell in A.A. Boddy's church in Sunderland in 1908 one of the people who flocked to witness the pentecostal outpouring was Bill Huchieson an elder of the Kilsyth Church. This visit, together with the fact that A.A. Boddy made a timely visit to Scotland, generated a hunger in the hearts of a number of the Church of God leaders for an outpouring of God's Spirit. On 1 February 1908, the fire fell.

Between thirty and forty were prostrated on the floor under the power of the Holy Spirit. Crowds flocked to the hall to see what was happening and those who could not get inside climbed up to the windows. In the weeks that followed two hundred people were baptised in the Spirit. Meetings were conducted every night of the week for four months. On a Sunday on which Cecil Polhill preached, twenty-eight young people offered themselves for missionary service. The Church of God, Kilsyth became Scotland's first Pentecostal congregation.

* I am indebted to James Huchieson, author of the definitive work on the history of Kilsyth, *Weavers, Miners and the Open Book* for much of the historical detail mentioned in this article.

Distinctives

Vaughan Roberts

ISBN 1-85078-331-4

In a fresh and readable style, the author of *Turning Points*, Vaughan Roberts, issues a challenging call to Christians to live out their faith. We should be different from the world around us – Christian distinctives should set us apart in how we live, think, act and speak. Targeting difficult but crucial areas such as our attitude to money and possessions, sexuality, contentment, relativism and service, this is holiness in the tradition of J.C. Ryle for the contemporary generation.

- Will you take up the challenge?

- Will you dare to be different?

Vaughan Roberts is Rector of St Ebbe's Church, Oxford. He is a popular conference speaker and University Christian Union speaker.

OM
publishing

He Walked Among Us
Evidence for the Historical Jesus

Josh McDowell & Bill Wilson

ISBN 1-89893-887-3

You've heard it (or asked it) yourself: "How do we know Jesus ever lived, and if He did live, what was He like?" The often repeated assertion is, "The only historical references to Him are contained in biased Christian sources."

- Expertly written by one of the world's most foremost Christian apologists, Josh McDowell (author of *Evidence That Demands a Verdict* & *The Resurrection Factor)* and writer-researcher, Bill Wilson.

- An opportunity to meet the real Jesus of history and know, without a doubt, that 'He walked among us.'

- Excellent resource for Christians to use in breaking down Hollywood impressions of Jesus Christ and confront sceptics who contend that Jesus never lived or that that He was not the Son of God.

alpha